Refugees, Gender and

Ellen Lammers

REFUGEES, GENDER AND HUMAN SECURITY

A theoretical introduction
and annotated bibliography

International Books, 1999

© Ellen Lammers / AGIDS-INDRA, 1999

ISBN 90 5727 028 5

Cover photographs: Nicole Teuwsen (Kampala, Uganda and
Reception Centre for Asylumseekers, Leiden, The Netherlands)
Cover design: Marjo Starink
DTP: Hanneke Kossen
Printing: Haasbeek

International Books, Alexander Numankade 17, 3572 KP Utrecht, The Netherlands,
tel.: +31-30-2731840, fax.: +31-30-2733614, e-mail: i-books@antenna.nl

ACKNOWLEDGMENTS

There are several people I wish to say thank you to for contributing to this publication.

Joke Schrijvers for initiating the project and for her kind and cooperative supervision during the months I worked on it.

Ton Dietz, director of AGIDS, for supporting the project.

Brigitte Holzner, Cindy Horst and Joke Schrijvers for their critical and helpful comments on earlier drafts of the theoretical introduction.

Diny and Joop Lammers for checking my English.

Olivier Briet, Mylène van Irsel, Brigitte Lammers, Hanneke Ronnes and especially Nicole Teuwsen for their much needed, last minute practical assistance in getting the annotated bibliography finished in time.

Thank you

Contents

Acknowledgments 5

Preface 9

PART ONE
Theoretical Introduction:
Refugees, Gender and Human Security

Introduction 15

1 **Refugees and Refugee Studies** 21
   Refugees: a local or a global phenomenon? 21
   Labelling: refugees, returnees, internally displaced persons
   and stayees 27

2 **Gender** 33
   The concept of gender 33
   Refugees and gender 35

3 **Human Security** 45
   Introduction of the concept by the UNDP 45
   Human security within policy circles 47
   Human security within academic circles 50

4 **Bringing Together the Three:**
   Refugees, Gender and Human Security 55

Literature 65

PART TWO
Annotated Bibliography

Introduction 73

Annotated Bibliography 75

Subject Index 171

Curriculum Vitae 175

Preface

Refugees and refugee issues have become part and parcel of the everyday reality of people all over the world. The largest number of refugees and internally displaced people have to search for refuge in their own countries or regions in the South, where resources to support them are minimal. The small minority of refugees that manage to enter Europe, the USA, Canada or Australia, is confronted with an increasingly negative imagery about the 'dangerous refugee flow', and an intensifying bureaucratic system that dehumanises them by giving labels which more often than not construct categories of exclusion. Over the last decade policies in the North have been redefined to urge the unwanted guests to return to their 'own' countries where peace and security are a far cry.

The political construction of 'the refugee issue' as a rule ignores the fact that the conflicts which cause population movements have to be understood within the context of the history of colonisation, de- and re-colonisation, and globalisation. These processes have created enormous inequities in wealth and power, and consequently have increased competition, discrimination and exclusion not only between, but increasingly also within countries – between people belonging to different socio-economic, ethnic and religious groups. 'The refugee' does not exist. It is a dangerous and detrimental construct. People who have been uprooted are as diverse as any other group of individuals. They differ according to their personality, socio-economic background and status, gender, age, caste, ethnic and religious affiliation. This has important consequences, both for understanding what happens with refugees, and for policies and practices dealing with them.

The vastness and complexity of refugee issues demands theoretical reflection. This is precisely what this book offers. It provides a completely new perspective in linking together the concepts of refugees, gender and human security. Although these concepts are crucial for understanding key aspects of the contemporary situation, they have not been dealt with in one theoretical framework. In addition to presenting an innovative and useful perspective to the subject, the book provides an annotated bibliography which can be used as a guide to the extensive literature in this field. Its focus is on human beings: refugees, displaced people, returnees and stayees. By joining together the concepts refugees, gender, and human security this book makes an attempt to merge different discourses originating from different academic fields. Moreover, it outlines a focus that relates individuals and their practices to broader processes, such as the 'local' with the 'global'.

INDRA's[1] first involvement with refugee issues was through my own research among internally displaced people in Sri Lanka (1993 – present). Currently the theme of 'refugee issues in international perspective' is given a lot of attention in INDRA's research programme and educational activities. Two of INDRA's annual lecture series have been devoted to the subject of human displacement. The first series entitled Forced Migration: Development and the Refugee Crisis (1996/1997), and the second Globalisation, Development and Refugee Movements (1998/1999). Presently, there are four PhD students working in this field.

In April 1997, INDRA decided to set up an interdisciplinary network for academics based in the Netherlands and engaged in research on refugee issues. The idea was to create a forum for researchers to become acquainted with each other's work and to exchange ideas, knowledge and research experiences. International refugee issues demand an approach that brings together specialists from various fields and invites them to engage in dialogue. The quick and enthusiastic response to our initiative can be taken as a sign that the times were ripe to embark on this endeavour. The network currently consists of approximately 80 researchers – both (Ph.D.) students and senior researchers – from discip-

---

1 INDRA, the 'International Development Research Associates' is part of AGIDS, the Amsterdam Institute for Global Issues and Development Studies, of the University of Amsterdam, the Netherlands.

lines as diverse as anthropology, (cross-cultural) psychology/psychiatry, law, political science and international relations, geography, development studies, history and gender studies. Seven network meetings have been held and have taken on the format of a seminar. Researchers present their own projects for an engaged and critical audience.

At one of the first network meetings it was decided to organise an international conference. A steering committee was given the responsibility for the conceptualisation and organisation of the conference 'Refugees and the Transformation of Society: Loss and Recovery' (from 21 to 24 April 1999). This conference intends to provide an input to develop new trajectories of research and academic perspectives. By explicitly bringing together different fields that are all too often kept separate, the conference aims at creating innovative knowledge in the field of refugee studies. This process is informed by the specific histories, contexts, and conflicts that have led to forced migration. In addition it aims to stimulate critical reflection on (inter)national politics, since refugees are being used as pawns in the politics of shifting powers. It is in the context and in support of the above mentioned activities that this book was compiled.

This book on 'Refugees, Gender and Human Security' is urgently needed. I am sure that it will stimulate many academics and practitioners to rethink their work.

Joke Schrijvers
Amsterdam, February 1999

Part One

THEORETICAL INTRODUCTION: REFUGEES, GENDER AND HUMAN SECURITY

Introduction

The UNHCR estimates that world-wide 13,2 million people have fled their countries and that another 30 million can be designated as 'internally displaced' (UNHCR 1997). Globally the debate concerning refugees is one of the main debates in contemporary politics, and it is a controversial one. Most European countries express a fear of being flooded by refugees from 'elsewhere' and consequently they are eager to close their borders or at least apply increasingly stricter rules for granting asylum. This has involved attempts to harmonise policy through various agreements on asylum seekers on the part of he European Union. Refugees from Africa, Asia or the Middle East, it is more and more commonly argued, should be accommodated within their own region. At the time of writing, the arrival of asylum seekers in the Netherlands is one of the hottest items in the Dutch news, discussed on a daily basis on television and in the newspapers, and displayed as an emergency situation – an emergency, one cannot escape the suggestion, for Dutch society.

Of the many issues involved in the refugee crisis, the international debate has predominantly focussed on the politico-legal ones, which is reflected in the media coverage of the 'problem'. When talking and writing about plane loads of asylum-seekers arriving in the Netherlands, the Dutch media limit their focus to issues pertaining to the Dutch legal system for refugees and immigrants. Time and again I am painfully surprised about the minimum of attention that is being paid to, for example, the political, economic and cultural backgrounds from which these people fled, or the personal implications that flight and exile have for people in all stages of life. Reducing the debate to this single aspect of politics and law though, carries in it the danger of forgetting what in fact is at stake: people who suffer because they cannot be at home. Edward

Said's statement that "to be rooted is perhaps the most important and least recognised need of the human soul" (1990: 364) suggests the pain bound to be felt by the majority of these forty-five million uprooted people. Part of that pain is people's struggle with issues like poverty, health, physical security, loss of friends and family, and disrupted security networks. Therefore, I believe, the narrow global focus with which refugee situations are approached, must be broadened and deepened. One important way of attaining this, is through academic studies of various types and disciplines – and where possible in active dialogue with refugees, policy makers and practitioners.

Nobody will deny that the refugee crisis is part and parcel of contemporary world politics. However, it is most important to realise that as long as people have been living together, they have also moved around searching for better or safer homes, sometimes willingly, but more often forced. Forced migration as such is thus not new to human experience. Nor is the defensive, and often outright offensive, reaction to people who arrive in a new country or territory by those already living there. In her book *Strangers to ourselves* Kristeva (1991) makes a journey through the historic images of 'the foreigner' to show how previous centuries have laid the foundation for our contemporary notion of 'foreigner' as endowed with legal meaning. She emphasises that the Enlightenment and the French Revolution have both generated an abundance of ideas about such concepts as nation and foreigners, although the first indication of a distinction in legal status was already present in the late Roman Empire in its discrimination between Romani and Barbari. By now, she argues, we have deeply internalised a specific national political consciousness: "we consider it normal that there are foreigners, that is, people who do not have the same rights as we do" (1991: 103). Refugees, in the late 20th century, are the most visible example of these. The very legal concept of 'the refugee' as we know it now, however, evolved in *this* century with the disintegration of empires and the rise of states in Europe – and the conflicts and wars these processes involved (Harrell-Bond 1988; Malkki 1995; Skran 1992; Zolberg et al. 1989). Drawing on the principal publications on the subject, Harrell-Bond's paper *Refugees and the international system: the evolution of solutions* (1995) provides a clear and succinct picture of the (legal) solutions to the refugee problem as developed since the inter-war period and up to the 1990s. It shows how refugees represent a fundamental tension and conflict in international politics: that of the sovereignty of nation states and their political imperatives as opposed to that of international humanitarian obligations. Furthermore, the paper and the literature it draws on reveal how refugee policy and legal solutions changed in focus from permanent solutions to durable (read: temporary) ones with the 'source' of refugees shifting from Europe during the World Wars to the countries of the South in subsequent decades. In the 1951 UN Convention Relating to the Status of Refugees – which was drafted on the basis of the experiences of the War and the situation of millions of displaced Europeans – refugees were defined as *individuals* who had a 'well-founded fear of persecution for reasons of race, religion, nationality, membership of a particular social group or political opinion'. Resettlement and naturalisation were seen as the solutions, based on the ideal of free movement and the economic benefits that refugees and migrants could bring to host countries. Consequently, most European refugees were considered *prima facie* refugees in practice, and almost without exception received permanent status in their new countries of residence. Repatriation was not referred to unless in negative terms, i.e. states were forbidden to *refoule* people to their country of origin (Harrell-Bond 1995: 5).[1] Later, as a result of the rapid de-colonisation in the 1960s, the many civil wars in newly independent countries that followed, and the "global consolidation of processes of

---

1 In their introduction to *When refugees go home*, Allen and Morsink add an interesting perspective to this issue of repatriation. They write: "The initial UN resolutions appertaining to refugees had explicitly mentioned voluntary repatriation as a first solution, and mass returns had occurred in Europe in 1945. But from 1947 until the 1970s it was effectively set aside as a means of resolving the plight of refugees. This was because discussion about it at international meetings was bound up with the far-reaching political implications of the creation of the state Israel and of the Cold War. Zionist demands for the right of repatriation to a Biblical homeland, and competing Palestinian demands to repatriate from their refugee camps, made debate about the general issue of returning refugees very sensitive. The fact that the United States and the Soviet Union took up opposed positions over the conflict, led to a stalemate situation" (1994: 2-3).

extraction and impoverishment" (Malkki 1995: 503), the developing countries of the Third World became the major 'source' of refugees, and the refugee phenomenon could no longer be considered a European problem. The 1951 Convention was extended by the 1967 Protocol to remove the Eurocentric geographical restrictions and include all world citizens. Soon after, refugees became identified as a 'Third World problem' to be resolved in these very regions (Zolberg et al. 1989). It was also then that the focus within refugee legalisation shifted from permanent to temporary solutions. From the 1980s onward voluntary repatriation, through 'tripartite agreements' with governments, has been promoted as the ideal solution for the cohort of refugees from the South. Legislation and UNHCR policy have been amended accordingly through concepts as the 'safe country' and the 'first country of asylum'. By far the largest numbers of refugees today still come from the poorest countries in the South, and again the majority of these have no choice but to search for refuge in their own regions. The relatively small group of refugees that manages to enter Europe, the USA, Canada or Australia, is confronted with ever-restricting policies that include a confusing array of different kinds of refugee statuses applied to them, often temporary in nature. Important to note is that this has also affected refugees from the former Yugoslavia (Harrell-Bond 1995). The curtailing effects this has on the security position and the well-being of today's refugees are harsh and manifold, and yet to be assessed.

Although some will rightfully argue that the refugee crisis as we know it today – with its specific legal, demographic and geographical aspects – is exclusively a sign of modern times, I wish to stress once more that forced migration as a human experience is *not*. I believe it is crucial to acknowledge the historical dimensions of 'refugeeness' so as to challenge its alleged novelty and 'abnormalness' – an adjective often projected on the people involved. For this purpose also we need to do away with the functionalist view of society that, to quote Malkki, "constructs displacement as an anomaly in the life of an otherwise 'whole', stable, sedentary society" (1995: 508). The perspective of history may help us realise that, as Allen put it poignantly, "Movement is normal. It is the frontier that is peculiar" (cited in Ranger 1994: 287).

Considering the pervasive presence of refugees all over the world, and the political and human issues this reality evokes, it seems more than relevant and fitting that refugee studies as an academic field of study has been establishing itself. Until the early 1980s there were few academics involved in studying the subject of forced migration. Moreover, most of the work that was produced, was directed by the needs of humanitarian agencies for data which would improve the logistics of their assistance programmes (Harrell-Bond 1988; Malkki 1995). Harrell-Bond suggests that part of the reason for this lack of academic attention to refugee issues, was informed by the reluctance of scholars to engage in the study of what they considered an ephemeral phenomenon. That refugee situations are not ephemeral but on the contrary involve long-term processes and practices, can no longer be denied. More and more often civil wars that produce large numbers of refugees – especially in Africa – continue over protracted periods of time; and equally important the personal, social and economic effects that refugeeness has for the people experiencing it, are all but short-lived. In 1982 the Refugee Studies Programme was established at Oxford University, UK, to start promoting multi-disciplinary academic study and documentation of forced migration.[2] Since 1988 the *Journal of Refugee Studies* has been the principal platform for publications and a source of information about the scholarly developments in this field of study. More recently, research programmes and institutes for refugee studies are being set up in the South – the very part of the world where after all by far the largest refugee populations both come from and reside.

The publication in hand, which comprises a theoretical introduction followed by an extensive annotated bibliography, aims at focusing on two aspects pertaining in many different ways to every single refugee or returnee situation, namely gender issues and issues of human security. In the theoretical introduction the three central concepts – refugees, gender and human security – will be discussed and placed within the

---

2　At around the same time, the Refugee Documentation Project was established at York University, Toronto, Canada, which also marked the start of the quarterly *Refuge*.

contemporary academic debates on refugee issues. In the last chapter they will be taken together and their mutual linkages and importance in relation to each other will be put forward. Inherent to this discussion are the arguments why I believe this bibliography is timely and needed, and how its focus contributes to the field of refugee studies. The choices that have been made as to what kind of publications were to be included in the annotated bibliography, and the descriptors that were used for finding these publications, will be outlined in a short introduction to the annotated bibliography.

CHAPTER 1

REFUGEES AND REFUGEE STUDIES

Refugees and forced migration have been pressing subjects of academic attention for about two decades now. From its inception, the bureaucratic domain of the 'international refugee regime' (Zolberg et al. 1989) – UN bodies in particular, but also governmental and non-governmental organisations – has played an influential role in determining and shaping the questions and assumptions that were taken and tackled by academics involved in studying refugee situations. As much as ten years ago, Harrell-Bond stressed the need for independent research that would not place 'uncritical reliance' on the statements, documents and literature produced by humanitarian agencies (1988: 2). This, I believe, has meanwhile been widely acknowledged, and refugee studies seems to have become an academic domain of research and knowledge-making in its own right. In this chapter I will focus attention on two subjects within the broad research field of refugee studies. The first will be the issue of how to approach the study of refugees, that is, as a local or as a global phenomenon. Secondly, I will deal with issues concerning the labelling of refugees and the fluidity of categories of people involved in processes of forced migration. The rationale for choosing exactly these two issues out of so many urgent ones, is inspired by the links that both issues have with gender and human security, the concepts central to this publication.

Refugees: a local or a global phenomenon?

Being trained as an anthropologist with a particular interest in people's individual thoughts, feelings and aspirations, I am personally inclined to focus attention in research on the local level authenticity of events and situations. As regards refugees, without doubt a lot can be learned from anthropological studies of refugee situations or communities, as these studies – when done thoroughly – will make visible in depth the local dynamics of a refugee situation in all its possible complexities and contradictions (*see in Part Two: Davis 1992; Harrell-Bond & Voutira 1992; Kearney 1995; Malkki 1995*).[3] Focusing on a single locality when studying refugees, has, I believe, two principal advantages. Firstly, it will foster an understanding of the 'diversity within'. Far too often the label of 'refugee' artificially constructs and degrades people into a one-dimensional, homogeneous category. Reality, however, shows that 'refugees' have many different identities, differentiated along many dimensions, such as gender, age, socio-economic-, ethnic- and regional background, or caste. Except for their common experience of having felt forced to migrate, they are an extremely heterogeneous category of people. This question will be elaborated upon in the next section on labelling and fluid categories. Secondly, it is of crucial importance to see and acknowledge the agency and creativity that people tend to reveal, especially when faced with extremely dire living circumstances. Refugees often show a remarkable ability to 'make do' when faced with material as well as non-material dilemmas and emergencies. In order to do justice to refugees' extraordinary capabilities, it is high time that the 'dependency-myth', which has so often been applied to refugees, be invalidated (Harrell-Bond 1986) (*see in Part Two: Allen 1996; Allen & Morsink 1994; Harrell-Bond, Voutira & Leopold 1992; Kibreab 1993*). This may be most successfully done through long-term, located studies of people's daily life struggles and the strategies they develop to make a living in the broadest sense of the word. Both academic understanding and practical relief support can be improved by taking into account the specific and personal histories, contexts, and conflicts that have led to people's displacement. One example of such a study is the paper by Harrell-Bond and Wilson (1990) included in the bibliography of Part Two, which explores how an anthropological understanding of death could inform the

---

3 References in italics in the main text refer to examples of related publications included in the annotated bibliography of Part Two.

provision of relief programmes for bereavement and burial so as to make a psycho-social contribution to the welfare of refugees as well as improve administrative and health issues.

The above argument, however, at the same time calls for awareness of its flip-side. If we were to locate the impacts of flight, exile and return *exclusively* in the personal or local realm, that would unjustly obscure the fact that human displacement nowadays has the status of a global phenomenon. This global phenomenon of 'refugeeness' both influences and is influenced by larger constellations of sociopolitical, cultural and environmental processes and practices (Loescher 1993; Malkki 1995; Zolberg et al. 1986). Moreover, studies dealing with particular refugee communities should be imbedded in critical reflection on (inter)national politics *because* we see refugees and constructions of 'the refugee' increasingly being used as pawns in the politics of shifting powers – locally, nationally and internationally (*see in Part Two: Kibreab 1996; Schrijvers 1997; Scott-Villiers et al. 1993; Weighill 1997; Xenos 1993*). Scholars in the field of international relations applying foreign policy analysis (FPA) to refugee studies, deal with the issues pointed at here. In short the questions they try to answer, are: how do foreign policies affect forced migration and vice versa? and, how do nation states use population displacement as an instrument of foreign policy? Elizabeth Ferris (1993) is outspoken in asserting that, while several studies show how foreign policies have influenced *responses* to refugee flows, hardly any scholarly attention is being paid to the reality that foreign policies are often nothing less than responsible for *creating* refugee flows. As for this lack of attention Zolberg et al. (1986) and Loescher (1992, 1993) are two of the exceptions, since they focus on the issue of how international factors, both directly and indirectly, infringe on and often exacerbate social and violent conflicts that trigger refugee flows – especially in the South. Refugees, Loescher (1992) puts it bluntly, have become instruments of warfare and military strategy. Indeed, there are plenty of examples of how during the Cold War superpower conflicts were fought out in Third World countries, especially in countries with internal revolutionary conflicts.

The thirty-year war between Eritrea and Ethiopia serves as one poignant example. Until 1974 the Ethiopian imperial regime managed to contain the separatist uprising in Eritrea – backed by several Arab states, including Sudan – with large-scale military and financial assistance from the United States and Israel. However, when the Mengistu regime took over after the revolution in 1974, the picture almost turned round: the Soviet Union and Cuba now came to Ethiopia's rescue, while the United States turned a friendly face towards the Eritreans. To make things even more complicated, conflicts within the Arab world contributed to the internal strife within the Eritrean liberation movement, which was partly a strife between Muslims and Christians (Papstein 1991; Pateman 1990; Zolberg et al. 1986). Since Eritrea's independence in 1993, the options Eritrean returnees have had for tackling the multiple issues of (in)security upon return, have still been partly determined by the macro-level processes in which their lives are embedded. Painfully illustrative is that international donors have been most reserved in making funds available for reintegration and rehabilitation programmes in Eritrea, because, so various authors suggest, with the end of the Cold War the region is no longer such a strategically important area (Allen 1996; Kibreab 1996). It therefore does not come as a surprise that any active attention to the renewed eruption of violence between both countries last spring, has received meagre international support. The predicament of Eritrean and Ethiopian refugees has been shaped by national, regional and global contextual factors alike – and continues to be so.

One example of how a nation state used its refugee policy as an instrument of foreign policy, is put forward by Loescher (1992), where he describes the position Pakistan took during the war between the Soviet Union and Afghanistan. By providing refuge for millions of Afghan refugees and by providing a channel for the free flow of weapons to the anti-communist guerrillas based there, Pakistan strengthened its relations with the United States, and was in turn rewarded with substantial US military and economic assistance. Refugee policy is used in a slightly different way, when the aim of containing the number of refugees entering a country is put forward as justification for certain foreign policy measures that may in actual fact have different objectives in mind. So the French government has justified its support for the military *junta* in Algeria, by telling the public that a possible take-over by the Muslim fundamentalists would most certainly effectuate a mass influx of Algerian refugees to France.

There are, however, also less direct ways in which external factors influence the many internal conflicts that 'produce' refugees, than the more or less straightforward foreign policies mentioned above.[4] Our late 20th century 'global village', Zolberg et al. put it bluntly, "is founded on enormous asymmetries of power and wealth, and exhibits distinctively anomic features" (1986: 157). Indeed it cannot be denied that part of the structural distortions – both economic and political – that continue to disturb future developments in many poor countries, stem from their incorporation into the global economic system on disadvantageous terms. An important question is how this fits the debate on globalisation, and in particular its discussions about homogenisation versus heterogenisation (Appadurai 1990; Kloos 1997). Sassen (1997) argues that while economic globalisation de-nationalises national economies, (forced) migration re-nationalises politics. What she alludes to is that human displacement often provokes discourses of 'self and other' that seem to contrast sharply with the notion of globalisation as referring to the intensification of a consciousness of the world as a whole (Robertson 1990). In fact, nation states increasingly 'defend' their territory against newcomers, especially refugees. Interesting in this respect is that "the definition of refugees in general international law embodies an 'internalist' vision whose validity is challenged by contemporary [global] realities" (Zolberg et al. 1986: 151). Not only are the conflicts and violence forcing someone to flee, assumed to lie within the borders of the refugee's country of origin – with little or no concern for the location of the causes of the conflict – but also, as Malkki (1995) puts it, does the legal apparatus concerned with refugees tend to take the contemporary order of sovereign nation states as given. She herself argues in favour of a "denaturalizing, questioning stance to-

---

4 The point must be made that foreign policies are not necessarily rational, straightforward or consistent, as they are the outcome of processes of negotiation and competition between different bureaucracies and institutions within and outside the borders of a nation state. In other words, no government or state is a unitary actor (Light 1994).

ward the national order of things" (1995: 517) as this may identify new research directions as regards refugees and forced migration as well as new forms of political engagement and action. The crux of it all would be, I believe, that a different way of thinking about borders and boundaries when actually dealing with refugees – i.e. trying *not* to think them – may effect inclusion and relative security instead of exclusion and outright insecurity for people who have been forced – due to a complex mix of internal *and* external factors – to flee their homeland. Or, in Malkki's own words, "if we accept that poverty, political oppression and mass displacement of people are all global or world-systemic phenomena, then it becomes difficult to localize them (and to localize refugees, specifically) in the Third World" (1995: 503).

Two lines of thought run through this section. The first makes an argument for localised research and action, informed by knowledge of the specific and personal histories, contexts, and conflicts that have led to flight. According to the second line of thought "to the extent that the causes are international, the solutions too require actions at the international level" (Zolberg et al. 1986: 167). Not surprisingly, both have a point in case. For our world, therefore, where a 'generalised condition of homelessness' seems the rule rather than the exception (Malkki 1992; Schrijvers 1997) what we need is a better understanding of the *interplay between local and (trans)national* discourses of antagonism and the subsequent exclusion of individuals and communities from a life of material and non-material well-being. In my search for literature, however, it soon became clear that there are very few studies that aim at this dual understanding – or even better, that manage to acquire or portray it (*see in Part Two: Malkki 1994; Mazur 1989; Menjivar 1993; Shami 1996*). This finding may have been reinforced by my particular search direction, which was dominated by the concern with gender issues. After all, gender is usually dealt with either in a theoretical, abstract way or as a local phenomenon. Anticipating what will be argued in chapter four, I wish to stress even at this point that an interdisciplinary dialogue is crucial if it is indeed beyond the scope of one particular research project to acquire a dual understanding of local and global factors pertaining to every refugee situation. Ideally, therefore, many of the studies listed in this bibliography – studies that predominantly use the local framework – should in the future be embedded in a wider framework of interdisciplinary understanding and research.

Labelling: refugees, returnees, internally displaced persons and stayees

The title of this publication – *Refugees, Gender and Human Security* – it must be admitted, fails to cover one of the objectives that guided the compilation of the bibliography. This objective was to search for literature concerning *all* subjects of human displacement – refugees, returnees, internally displaced persons and stayees alike. The principal reason is obvious: almost all situations of human displacement – and especially those that take place over protracted periods of time – display a reality of complex and sometimes contradictory forces that urge people to make decisions on whether or not to leave, to stay, to cross a border, to cross it again. In the prevalent jargon, depending on what decision they take, people become either refugees, internally displaced persons, stayees or returnees. At the same time, however, both scholarly and humanitarian attention is almost exclusively oriented towards those who in the process become designated as refugees. This, I believe, is a most unfortunate result of what Allen and Turton call 'the tyranny of labels' (1996: 5). Why, if all four groups undergo and take part in the dilemmas and challenges of forced migration, has attention been so biased? The most straightforward answer is that refugees, those who have crossed an international border out of 'well-founded fear for persecution', are the only ones enjoying the ambiguous privilege of being legally defined through the 1951 UN Convention. Thus they are acknowledged, recognised and treated as a specific group of people enjoying specific rights – and being worth studying.

I believe this bias in attention should be put aside so that not only refugees, but also returnees, internally displaced persons and stayees receive both the scholarly and the humanitarian attention they deserve as actors in the processes of forced migration. As for returnees, academic attention has surely picked up in recent years. Especially worth mentioning are the two substantial publications that resulted from the 1980s UN-RISD research programme on repatriation in Africa: *When refugees go home* (Allen & Morsink (eds) 1994), and *In search of cool ground: war, flight & homecoming in Northeast Africa* (Allen (ed) 1996). In the introductions the editors put forward several reasons why repatriation has so long been ignored by scholars. They state that research on returnees has long been indirectly restricted by the nature of international thinking about repatriation (see introduction and footnote 1). They also refer to the more practical difficulties of studying returnees, which are closely related to the fact that they are often dispersed populations, left to their own devices and without a legally recognised status. Because repatriation often takes place in the unstable settings of the aftermath of war – or even while war is still raging – research, let alone long-term research, is often simply impossible. As for so-called internally displaced people – who present by far the largest numbers of uprooted people in the world – this same reason of instability and insecurity may apply as to why they have received so little attention from researchers. As for humanitarian assistance to internally displaced persons – given the fact that they do not enjoy a legal definition that entitles them to certain international rights – this is generally made difficult due to the tendency of governments to resent any outside interest shown in their internally displaced populations, maintaining that it is an infringement on national sovereignty (Allen & Turton 1996). Lastly, people who in the upheavals of war or drought decide not to flee, or those who have no choice but to stay put, appear to be altogether left out from research on forced migration (see Malkki 1995: 515-516).

While arguing in favour of bringing to light the particular experiences and problems of returnees, internally displaced persons and stayees, I hasten to add that it is not my intention to argue for a stricter conceptual categorisation of the different groups. Instead, I believe that these categories often fail to reflect real life circumstances, and apart from being non-applicable they share in the harmful effect that processes of labelling can have for the people involved.

In his article *Labelling refugees: forming and transforming a bureaucratic identity* (1991) Zetter examines how and with what consequences people become labelled as refugees, how their identities are formed and transformed consequently, as well as how these identities are manipulated in public policy and bureaucratic practices. Within the current expanding 'refugee regime' these are very important issues. As will become clear in the course of this theoretical introduction, the issue of politicised labels bestowed on refugees and other subjects of forced migration, has several linkages to the subject of human security. An indication of some of these will be outlined below. Important to bear in mind always when dealing with 'the refugee label' is the fact that this label is not just definitional, and certainly not neutral or precise, but instead conveys explicit values and judgements.

The first point in case is that the refugee label enforces a stereotyped identity of 'the refugee'. Many studies confirm what seems self-evident, namely that refugees conceive their identity quite differently from those bestowing the label (*in Part Two see: Harrell-Bond 1986; Hitchcox 1990; Lutz 1991; Malkki 1996*). In other words, the refugee label disregards the 'diversity within' – the differences according to, for example, age, ethnicity, gender, economic and educational background that exist among people labelled as refugees and allegedly belonging to one homogeneous category. In fact, the identity of uprooted people by definition is all but one-dimensional and often shows further complexities due to the changing circumstances they find themselves in. A formerly highplaced person, for example, may struggle with a fall in social status when being forced to live in a refugee settlement without his or her former status being recognised by other refugees, let alone by foreign relief agencies. Also, as will be put forward in the next chapter, gender identities may change as a result of women's and men's differential experiences of living in exile. For these reasons alone, one should never speak of 'the refugee experience' and similarly the label 'refugee' will never do justice to the multiplicity of experiences and identities that uprooted people deal with.

However, there is not only a definitional problem. In defining refugees as one stereotyped group of people, time and again the message is conveyed directly or indirectly of their helplessness and their identity as victims of external forces. Or, as Zetter puts it, "... an individual identity is replaced by a stereotyped identity with a categorical prescription of assumed needs" (1991: 44). This victim-identity does not do justice to reality nor to the strength that people display in the dire circumstances of exile, and as such it denies their human dignity. Moreover, starting from this victim-identity, many relief agencies have disregarded refugees' own perceptions, skills and resources in the planning and implementation of relief operations, which has often resulted in the failure of for example settlement projects for self-sufficiency. Holding on to their own preconceived assumptions about refugees, agencies have often found themselves painfully surprised by what they consider incongruent behaviour of refugees towards their institution's actions and programmes (Harrell-Bond 1986; Waldron 1988; Zetter 1991).

The issue of a stereotyped identity furthermore bears relevance to what was said above about conceptually separated categories of refugees, returnees, internally displaced persons and stayees. These labels often fail to reflect how people see themselves, nor do they take into account cultural and historical patterns of movement and the arbitrariness of national frontiers for people 'on the move' (Allen & Turton 1996; Malkki 1995; Ranger 1994). The current jargon concerning forced migration is very much based on a (western) 'sedentarist bias', which takes the attachments of people to certain places and territories as a given fact, as well as the national order of sovereign nation states (Malkki 1995; Stepputat 1994). In many cases this approach has effected harmful consequences for the people involved. As for internally displaced people, the fact that they are not recognised by the 1951 UN Convention as refugees has serious repercussions for their material and non-material security position. The definition of their rights becomes highly politicised and arbitrarily dependent on the local, regional and international politics related to their situation in a particular country. Schrijvers (1997) chooses to replace the term 'internally displaced persons' by 'internal refugees' so as to stress not only the nature of the situation these people find themselves in – which is refugee-like and often worse – but also the fact that they are *refugees* entitled to protection and support (*see in Part Two: Deng 1995; Kathina 1996; Lee 1996; Schrijvers 1997, 1999; Wilson 1992; Zlotnik 1990*). At the same time, in-depth analyses of actual situations of war and internal displacement can no longer bypass the fact that the boundaries between people who are actively involved in war, and those belonging to 'civil society' are often very obscure. Not only the mutually exclusive categories of refugees, returnees and internally displaced people are invalid, but it has also often proved non-sensical to distinguish between refugees and locals in the same area. Because the way people are labelled determines the assistance they will receive, distinctions between refugees and locals can create enmity between both groups, and as such destabilise the co-existing ethnicities of locals (hosts) and refugees (Zetter 1991). Moreover, the unjustly selective provision of assistance based on inappropriate though institutionally determined labels, may result in outright disasters for the people involved (*see in Part Two: Harrell-Bond 1986; de Waal 1988*).

The above shows that the process of labelling is political and connected with issues of power and control. First of all, labelling appears to be an inescapable part of the bureaucratic requirements of the refugee regime. Relief agencies and the UNHCR use clearly earmarked funds to assist their target groups, and project managers are held responsible for how the money is spent. Consequently, bureaucratic interests and procedures are the determinants of how the refugee label is defined. And for refugees to be included in the assistance programmes designed for them, and to gain access to protection, food and other resources, requires their conformity to the label (Zetter 1991). This, some argue, leads to oppressive practices in refugee assistance, and forms part of an 'ideology of control' within aid programmes (Harrell-Bond, Voutira & Leopold 1992). Furthermore, the helplessness on the part of the victims of forced migration serves as a powerful image for the appeal for international funds. Also, this helplessness is used as a legitimisation for the exercise of control on the part of agencies and host governments. For the latter, the presence of refugees may furthermore serve political and economic ends. Kibreab (1993) describes how the Somali government intentionally kept refugees institutionalised and dependent on international aid so as to foster international attention for its cause of a united Somalia. Furthermore, this international attention ensured a continued flow of funds and economic resources into the country (Girardet 1981). In other words, refugees can be 'big business' for both (inter)national relief agencies and host governments.

A last important point must be added to the arguments above. Having highlighted the unjust practice of labelling refugees as helpless and dependent, it would be contradictory to portray these same people as being defencelessly at the mercy of the labels bestowed on them by outsiders. By means of labelling people, agencies control their access to food, shelter and medical care. However, the flip-side is also true: people can actively *use* their label in order to gain access to these and other resources – and in many circumstances they do. A friend of mine in Uganda, for example, told me how she lied to an agency responsible for the repatriation of Ugandans from Sudan. By convincing them she was a Ugandan refugee wanting to go home, she in actual fact ensured her flight as a Sudanese refugee to Uganda. In other words, the practice of labelling in many situations presents a complex and delicate blend of oppressing people and of providing them with a tool for empowerment at the same time. This empowerment is not only related to direct material gains. Also, as Zetter suggests, "A 'refugee consciousness' maintains an identity, and the enhanced solidarity may be turned to advantage as a lever on governments and agencies" (1991: 55).

CHAPTER 2

GENDER

The concept of gender [5]

The concept of gender was introduced in social science – and feminist studies in particular – in the early 1980s. It has by now become a well-known concept that enjoys wide usage in different disciplines, as well as outside the walls of academia. The most basic definition of gender refers to the social construction of femininity and masculinity as culturally and historically specific. On top of that gender is generally supposed to refer to existing power relations between men and women. These power differentials may be culturally worked out by means of prescribed gender roles and are usually connected with a more implicit power structure of gender symbolism.

It is not the aim of this publication to go into detailed description and discussion of gender theory in general. Nevertheless, I judge it helpful and necessary to contextualise the gender concept by presenting in brief some headlines of feminist theory, in which the concept has always been embedded. The primary reason for doing so is that this bibliography intends to focus on the theoretical, academic studies that combine refugee studies and gender issues, rather than on policy documents that deal with gender in terms of the actual needs and problems of particular groups of refugee women. The latter kind of documents and statements, unquestionably of the utmost importance, can be found in at least three other substantial bibliographies (*see in Part Two: UNHCR 1985, 1989; Neuwirth & Vincent 1997*).

---

5   I wish to acknowledge the contributions to this section by Cindy Horst.

Feminist theory from the start has been deeply involved in a search for an epistemological foundation of its own (Grant 1993). Three mutually related epistemological issues that have been, and still are, in the forefront of feminist theory will be briefly outlined below for the relevance they bear to the central arguments of this chapter on refugees and gender.[6] These particular epistemological issues – deconstruction, situating knowledges, and representation – have been much influenced by postmodern and post-structuralist thinking.

To start with, feminist theory has always occupied itself with challenging the taken-for-granted categories and conceptions that underlie mainstream scientific research. Gender categories, commonly presented as if based on a supposedly 'natural' relation between the sexes, were the first to be challenged and deconstructed by feminist researchers. The exercise was inspired by the finding that scientific categories, and science in general, were based on an implicit though unmistakably male bias – as they still largely are. In their pledge for deconstructing existing (scientific) categories, feminists have concerned themselves particularly with so-called binary oppositions (man-woman, male-female, subject-object) as these unjustly make the world appear fixed and classifiable into mutually exclusive positions. Special attention was paid to women's subjectivity, which, as some feminists argue, is systematically defined *in relation to* men. Irigaray is outspoken in her statement that women are denied an identity of their own, and are instead defined in opposition to the masculine norm (in Chanter 1998).

This male bias – getting on to the second issue – feeds on an essentialist conception of knowledge and truth that feminist researchers want to do away with. They radically challenge the mainstream idea of objectivity in science that is based on the mind/body dichotomy. The

---

6 It must be emphasised that 'feminist theory' is not a coherent and unitary field of study. Feminist theory has developed and changed over time, and moreover there are multiple 'feminisms' across disciplines and across geographical regions. The three issues that I pose as central largely reflect my personal choice of what is relevant in the context of this publication. For substantial discussion of the developments within feminist theory, see Sandra Harding (1986) and Judith Grant (1993).

Cartesian belief in a coherent and rational mind that produces (the one and only) objective scientific knowledge is to be rejected as incomplete and invalid, according to feminists. Knowledge is not produced by means of a neutral scientific gaze, but instead all knowledge is embodied and particular. This feminist viewpoint allows the incorporation of knowledge gained through the bodily and emotional aspects of experience. In brief: (post-modern) feminists argue for substituting the idea of a mastering and objective scientific 'Truth' by the conceptualisation of knowledge as being by definition partial, fluctuating and 'situated' (Haraway 1991). Social, historical and cultural dimensions of subjectivity should be articulated in these situated knowledges, or in other words, the researcher must account for her or his own 'situatedness' as well.

Closely linked to the feminist rejection of scientific objectivity, is its criticism of the remote relation in mainstream science between the knowing subject and his or her object of knowledge. The latter is often unjustly turned into 'a passive resource for appropriation' (Haraway 1991). Apart from the unethical aspects of such a representation, it is also false: knowledge is not simply 'out there' (Caplan 1988). Instead, knowledge is created by means of a dialectical and dialogical process of interaction and communication, in which all parties involved exert power (Schrijvers 1991). This requires a change in perspective towards the objects of knowledge, namely from passive resources to conscious agents.

Refugees and gender

How do these three rather abstract epistemological issues apply to the study of refugees, and why are they considered so important?

Deconstructing 'the refugee woman'

As regards the epistemological issue of deconstruction, I believe its importance lies in the first place in the room it leaves to acknowledge the fluidity and heterogeneity of categories such as refugees, or refugee women. Within feminist theory it has been rightfully argued that women are not just one 'thing', that they cannot be 'pinned down' (Chanter

1998). Moreover, a universalising approach towards women 'mutes' them and renders invisible critical aspects of diversity in experience and perception among them (Indra 1996). Therefore, instead of conceptualising and treating women as if they were a homogeneous category, the theoretical move from 'sameness' to 'difference' must be integrated into research (Moore 1988, 1994). This applies very much to the study of women refugees. As was argued in the previous chapter, the refugee label often has the negative and harmful effect of denying people's autonomous, personal identity. The problem, it must be added, is not the mere fact that classification or labelling exists, but the fact that it is used in a closed and hierarchical way (Horst 1998). As for the classification – or rather, stigmatisation – of refugees, it is the refugee *women* who are mostly worst off: they are, anonymously and homogeneously, depicted as the 'vulnerable cases', the most deplorable victims of forced migration. And yet it is obvious that refugee women see and experience a lot of differences among themselves – differences according to age, religion, personal character, cultural background, life experience, educational standard and marital status to name a few. It follows that there are also multiple different ways in which they deal with their realities of exile. It is therefore crucial that researchers appreciate and explore this heterogeneity, and avoid taking refugee women or their experiences as one. This deserves special attention because of the fact that, as Moghadam (1994) argues, constructions of masculinity and femininity are often blown up in times of war. General public perception often suggests that men become more aggressive than ever, and women more helpless. This, however, goes against observations that will be referred to below about changing gender roles and the strengths of women in insecure situations.

Another argument why one should not uncritically focus on mutually exclusive gender categories when studying refugees, can be taken from an article by Schrijvers, *Internal refugees in Sri Lanka: the interplay of ethnicity and gender* (1997). It shows how gender cross-cuts other divisions like ethnicity, age or class (see also Indra (1996)). Schrijvers, who carried out her research in the government camps in Colombo for Tamil and Muslim internal refugees, writes: "The longer the refugees were forced to live dependent lives, packed together in the camps like animals, the greater was their urge to (re)create structures and symbols which expressed their identity as human beings. Ethnicity and gender were the discourses most readily at hand and most easily moulded into organising principles" (1997: 73). She shows how Muslims and Tamils each and all in their own way used gender as an "ethnic marker". The Muslims applied a very strict gender discourse for the organisation of their camps in order to guard the honour of their community. In this way they emphasised their identity as Muslims in opposition to outside groups conceived of as 'the other' or 'the enemy'. Interestingly, the Tamils did not stress their ethnic identity when outside of the camps for safety reasons, but did do so within. Sexuality rules, marriage, and family relations were the gendered symbols through which the community's identity was reconfirmed – and at the same time re-negotiated by women and girls who could benefit from change (1997: 75-76). Referring back to these issues in a later article, Schrijvers (1999) concludes that in the Sri Lankan situation of internal refugees it is simply impossible to construct 'women' and 'ethnic groups' as separate analytical categories. The same issue is taken up in a somewhat different way by Meznaric (1994) in her article *Gender as an ethno-marker: rape, war and identity politics in the former Yugoslavia*. She examines two cases wherein women and their bodies have been pawns in male directed battles over ethnic identity, and argues that gender serves as an ethno-marker in boundary maintenance and in conflicts between groups.

Situated knowledge: refugees, gender and change

The practices of deconstructing alleged categories and situating knowledge are closely connected in feminist research. Both should serve as starting points in research about forced migration, because refugee situations provide many examples of allegedly fixed (gender) categories that prove flexible, and of former 'truths' about people and their (gendered) culture that prove changeable. This is the very theme dealt with elaborately in the papers in the volume *Reconstructing lives, recapturing meaning: refugee identity, gender, and culture change* (Camino & Krulfeld (eds) 1994).

Gender is always about power. Callamard (1992) argues that dramatic events occurring in people's lives can be factors that provoke or reinforce the transformation of gendered power structures. The changes in traditional gender relations that take place as a result of war, flight, exile or return provide vivid examples of these.

Refugee women and their dependants are commonly labelled as 'vulnerable groups'. Without wishing to deny the seriousness of their plight, I would like to stress that several studies have emphasised the extraordinary coping abilities of women refugees as compared to those of men (*see in Part Two: Kibreab 1995; McSpadden and Moussa 1993; Panos 1995; Schrijvers 1997; Spring 1979*). These studies explain how women refugees have managed to exert power and to re-negotiate their own positions within the hierarchical structures of their community. Other studies, it must be said, have largely reconfirmed the prevalent image of women refugees by showing how gender roles were not transformed in exile, but rather exacerbated with an increasing disadvantage for women as compared to men (*see in Part Two: Ager et al. 1995; Daley 1991*). These contradictory findings demonstrate the usefulness and interest of the epistemological concept of partial and situated knowledges. When applied to a gendered study of forced migration, it means that one should not take the vulnerability of women refugees as a matter of course, but rather examine it carefully in the specific location of their actual daily lives.

The situation of Eritrean refugees in Sudan serves as a typical example.[7] The impact of flight and exile on Eritrean women refugees has been diverse rather than unitary. Kibreab (1995) typifies these divergent experiences by referring to refugee women living in urban areas in Sudan as 'agents of change' and to those in rural settlements as 'sources of continuity'. At first instance this may sound as an invalid generalisation. However, several other studies (e.g. Bright 1992; Kuhlman 1990) also show that in the rural settlements in Eastern Sudan patriarchal relations were intensified – which for the women meant a greater degree of restriction and subordination than before – while many of those living in the

---

7 The studies from which the information for this example was taken, were all published before the renewed conflict between Ethiopia and Eritrea last year. Recent developments are therefore not mentioned in what is written below.

city of Khartoum managed to, and were compelled to, take on new responsibilities which effected changes in gender relations that instead gave them *more* freedom. If these refugees are ever to return to Eritrea, these experiences will undoubtedly influence their processes of repatriation. The new strength and resilience that many of the women built in exile – especially those who lived in urban areas – may prove powerful resources for their reestablishment and reintegration into the Eritrean society (Moussa 1995). Furthermore it can be expected that many of the former rural dwellers who became urbanised in Sudan will want to resettle in urban areas in Eritrea (Kibreab 1996). Habte-Selassie (1992) predicts that also many of those who lived in the large refugee settlements will want to return to towns in Eritrea, as they have become used to amenities and services like schools, clinics, running water and flour mills – a 'luxury' they do not wish to give up. However, one can reasonably assume that the choice returnees make for either village or town is influenced not only by assumptions regarding future material comfort, but also reflects changed personal perceptions of self and of one's place in the community. These certainly involve changes in gender relations and constructs. Bascom (1996) observes that indeed many returnees refer to the non-material advantages afforded by return. For some this may be embodied in the security they expect will be provided by kinship relations in former rural communities, whereas for others – especially women – the personal autonomy attained in exile, which they believe can only be preserved in urban areas, may be at the top of their lists.

It was mentioned briefly in the opening paragraph of this chapter that gender is defined theoretically not only as a cultural and symbolic construct but also as a social role and relationship (Moore 1988). These two understandings of gender should be linked in research in order to explore their interrelation in people's actual lives. Through such an approach researchers will be able to bring to the fore situations in which supposedly accepted gender constructs contrast with what men and women actually (can) do. That is another way of deconstructing the taken-for-granted and appreciating the fluidity of reality – and thus of knowledge. In the case of refugee and returnee situations particularly, this approach will generate very interesting information because the changing and transformative circumstances that refugees are in will account for tension and/or clashes between constructs and practice (*see in Part Two: Boddy 1995; Boone 1994; Buijs (ed) 1993; Callamard 1996; Chantanavich 1996*). Young and unmarried Somali girls, for example, are traditionally not supposed to work outside the home by themselves, as this spoils their – and thus the family's – honour. However, many of the Somali girls I met in Kampala eventually manage to come to the tailoring classes organised by the UNHCR, often after prolonged lobbying by the teacher with fathers, brothers and husbands. Admittedly, most of these girls return to the domestic arena immediately after their course has finished, but some succeed in setting up small businesses of their own in town. They are allowed to do so – or force permission – out of sheer survival necessity, but at the same time the traditional gender ideology is officially being upheld by (male) family members. The question remains what would happen to both the actual changes and the gender ideology in case of return to Somalia.

The above illustrates the overall point that because refugees by definition find themselves in a climate of change and transition – both personally, spatially and culturally – it would be naive to want to look for unchanging (academic) truths about their situation and experiences. Knowledge about refugees, internally displaced persons and returnees – how frustrating it may sometimes be for relief organisations – will always be changing and partial. The challenge for any researcher in the field of refugee studies is to recognise and appreciate this, and to situate his or her knowledge accordingly.

Representing refugee women

The last item for discussion is the connection between the third feminist epistemological issue mentioned – that of representation – and refugee studies. The argument has been put forward that the conceptual splitting up of researcher and researched is unjust as well as unreal, and must be avoided as much as possible. The 'objects of research' of mainstream science must be acknowledged and approached as subjects in their own right. After all, the process of research takes place in active dialogue and both researcher and researched are agents in the power-charged process of the production of knowledge. I regard this of utmost importance in research with refugees. Refugees are often seen as passive and dependent victims. Their agency is outright being denied when, for example, they are left to wait in long lines at different offices, being seen and treated as 'a refugee' in a homogeneous and anonymous group of people. The refugees I spoke to in Kampala, told me this treatment made them feel as if they were 'nothing', and kept explaining how it disgraced their dignity and self-respect. Researchers working with refugees must avoid making this mistake. First of all because it is unethical and harmful to deny a person's agency, and secondly because it does not depict reality. As I have argued before, refugees – and refugee women in particular – are far more actively in charge of their own lives than is commonly assumed and publicised. What Chanter (1998) says with regard to subjects in general, holds true for refugees and refugee women in particular: they are no "passive repositories" of power, they also 'make' power themselves.

With her study *Imposing aid: emergency assistance to* refugees (1986), Harrell-Bond was one of the first to explicitly put this issue to the fore. She shows how refugee images are powerfully imbued with a symbolism of helplessness, while her own suggestion is that this so-called 'dependency syndrome' is mainly caused by the anti-participatory manner in which humanitarian aid is provided. Indra (1996) observes that – since Harrell-Bond's landmark study – much more interest has been shown by researchers to adequately investigate and represent refugees' agency, and she adds that this clearly shows the influence of feminism in refugee studies (*see in Part Two: Van Esterik 1996; Gorashi 1997; Hitchcox 1990; Kibreab 1993; Madzokere 1993; Moussa 1993; Schrijvers 1997; Sullivan 1996; Tran 1993*).

However, the situation is not always straightforward. Schrijvers (1997) describes how in the camps for internal refugees in Colombo, women – unlike men – managed to retain the core of their gender identity, primarily because their role as mothers and caretakers for the family was not taken from them. In the restricting arena of the camps, men on the contrary lost most of their previous roles and their status. On top of that, many Tamil and Muslim women took up work outside the house, which made them co-providers for the family and gave them some previously unknown economic autonomy. However, Schrijvers continues, "... after becoming more familiar with the camps, I felt that in terms of power to control their own lives and community life in the camps, women were still on the losing end. Gradually I learned how vulnerable women were when it came to physical autonomy, especially when men were drunk. Wife beating, rape and forced pregnancies were not uncommon; in fact, all refugees who talked about this remarked that male 'domestic' violence linked to alcoholism was much more serious than it had been before. The men, even more than in 'normal' circumstances, tried to confine women's mobility and reduce their space of action in order to 'protect' and control them, especially if they were young and unmarried" (1997: 74). The dilemma Schrijvers struggles with refers back to what was said under the heading 'Deconstructing 'the refugee woman'': what representation of these women would do them justice most? Schrijvers wants to avoid reconfirming and reinforcing the image of refugee women as passive and lamentable victims which is habitually being publicised by NGOs, UN agencies and the media in general. On the other hand, constructing the image of refugee women as ever-strong and perfectly well able to look after themselves and their families, might take away the much-needed attention for their living circumstances and their gender-specific problems. Moreover, neither representation would be truthful to the complex reality the refugee women are in.

It is absolutely crucial that this issue of representation – who speaks of and for refugees, why, how, and with what consequences? – is taken seriously. Foucault (1972) showed that a will to knowledge and knowledge creation in itself, is also a will to power. And this power to define and classify is neither a disinterested nor an un-gendered one (Indra 1996). On the contrary, defining (or, representing) a category of people as 'the other', as 'insane', 'criminal' – as 'outsiders in our midst' – is in itself a way of controlling them, of setting them apart from mainstream society and thereby redefining what 'is and should be' (Foucault 1961). Unfortunately these exclusionary mechanisms apply very much to refugees. The more so, because the prevalent discourses on refugees stem largely from the "enormous, objective asymmetry of power and voice between state representatives, helpers, advocates and researchers on the one hand, and refugees on the other" (Indra 1996: 37; see also Ranger 1994). As for the asymmetry in power between researchers and researched, it sometimes proves very difficult to avoid. Schrijvers (1999) is faced with this problem during her research among internal refugees in Sri Lanka. She finds that in the direct presence of war the power relation between researcher and the subjects of research is likely to take on a different shape. For one thing, the researcher – unlike the researched – nearly always has the privilege of being able to 'retreat' once things get too nasty. Furthermore the research subjects – the refugees – may lose some negotiating power simply because the war silences them. Any piece of information given may be enough reason for them to fear for their lives. Indirectly, however, this situation also silences the researcher. Moore (1993), in her article about Khmer and Vietnamese refugee women in Thailand, describes her personal struggle with the contradiction she feels between being, as an American, a representative of the dominant power in the region while at the same time being vulnerable like all women to rape and assault in the lawless environment of the camp where she carries out her fieldwork.

It is true that theory and methods of research in situations of conflict and violence are still in a very premature state (Brandt 1996; Nordstrom and Robben 1995). Still, I believe that a feminist approach to refugee studies may have valuable contributions, as feminists in general share at the basis a deeply felt commitment to problematise and change existing, unequal power relations. This may be possible through a thorough commitment to understand the (diverse, changing) lived experiences of people, but also needs the critical unpacking of seemingly self-evident categories and relationships that is characteristic of (post-modern) feminism. Indra (1996) refers to an example of how this can have important practical consequences in refugee work and legislation. She mentions studies that show how it makes a difference to one's understanding of immigration and refugee policy whether a generalised view is taken or a gendered perspective. Through contesting the general category of 'refugee' many authors have been advocating against the male bias in refugee legislation and in favour of the inclusion of gender oppression as a criterion for official political/legal refugee status (*see in Part Two: Bhabha*

1996; Bissland 1997; Greatbach 1989; Indra 1989; Kelly 1994; Macklin 1996; Mahmud 1996; Spijkerboer 1994). The issue of gendered insecurity experienced by women refugees through sexual violence and harassment will be further dealt with in chapter four.

For me personally the idea behind academic involvement with gender issues in refugee situations is – be it indirectly or in the long run – the improvement of refugees' living circumstances and security positions as well as the appreciation of (women) refugees' multiple resources and strengths. I therefore hope that, as in the example of refugee legislation mentioned above, academic studies on refugees and gender will inspire changes for the better in the bureaucratic aid apparatus that currently characterises the 'refugee regime'. For this to materialise it is necessary that researchers dare to situate themselves and to take sides. As Schrijvers (1999) states quite rightly, especially in the circumstances of war and repression that refugees find themselves in, being neutral and a-political as a researcher indirectly means supporting the dominant regime.

Chapter 3

Human Security

In this chapter the last of the three concepts central to this bibliography – that of human security – will be introduced and critically discussed. This serves as reference for the next and last chapter, in which I will put forward how in my opinion the concept of human security can be best applied to (gendered) refugee studies and the advantages this may yield. In feminist studies it is often stressed that one needs to study the genealogy of concepts in order to be in a position to de- and reconstruct them (Braidotti 1994). That is the very aim of this third chapter.

Introduction of the concept by the UNDP

It is only recently that the concept of human security was introduced in policy and academic circles as a potential core concept for international issues of peace and development. Its first introduction was in the UNDP's Human Development Report of 1994. Here it was accompanied by the grand words that "The idea of human security, though simple, is likely to revolutionize society in the 21st century" (1994: 22). I am not sure what was envisaged by the word 'revolutionize' in this context, but the Report does show quite convincingly that – in theory – a lot can be had from working and thinking from the perspective of human security. The most interesting and important observation in my opinion concerns the meaning and content of the concept of security. The UNDP argues that the concept has long been interpreted too narrowly, focusing almost exclusively on security threats to nations caused by external aggression and/or the fear for a global nuclear war. The fact that security was related to nation-states rather than to people and their daily life insecurities implied, so it is argued, an unjust limiting of the concept.

Moreover, as security was related primarily to violence and warfare across national borders, many other aspects and forms of (in)security – economic, social, personal – were unjustly disregarded.

Having realised these limitations and biases, the UNDP concludes that 'time is ready' to make a transition from the narrow concept of national security to the all-encompassing concept of human security (1994: 24). The proposed conceptual shift is linked to the argument – or belief – that 'the world' in the mid 1990s may be ready for an "entirely new vision" and a "profound transition", comparable to the watershed of new initiatives and actions in the mid 1940s. The end of the Second World War, the birth of the United Nations, the introduction of the Marshall Plan and the Bretton Woods institutions, and the widespread liberation movements in the colonies are mentioned as examples of the great transition now fifty years ago. Events and circumstances that trigger the belief voiced by the UNDP in a similar transition in the mid nineties, are: the end of the Cold War and subsequent democratic transitions in formerly communist societies, a steady fall in global military expenditures, the opening up of economies world wide and the prospects for peace in South Africa and the Middle East (1994: 5). The comparison, it seems to me, is arguable. Interesting information to be added is that this Human Development Report was written in preparation for the World Social Summit for Social Development (Copenhagen, March 1995) – and that this coincided with the 50th anniversary of the United Nations. Reason enough in itself, one would think, to look for 'revolutions' and 'entirely new visions'.

Human security: the UNDP definition

This new concept of human security introduced by the UNDP in 1994, is based on a United Nations old time credo – freedom from fear and freedom from want. In defining security, the UNDP argues, one should avoid equating human security with human development. Human development is a broader concept, defined as the process of widening the range of people's choices. Human security is related to this, as security means that people can exercise their choices safely and freely, and with relative confidence that the opportunities they have today are not completely lost tomorrow (UNDP 1994: 23). Aspects of and threats to human security are subsumed under seven – partly overlapping – categories (1994: 24-33):

1 Economic security: threats of unemployment, job insecurity, bad working conditions, income inequalities, inflation, insufficient social security networks and homelessness.

2 Food security: problems with regard to physical and economic access to food.

3 Health security: threats to health and life from infectious and parasitic diseases, HIV and other viruses, diseases through polluted air or water and insufficient access to health services.

4 Environmental security: degradation of local and global ecosystems, water scarcity, floods and other natural disasters, deforestation and the pollution of water, air and soil.

5 Personal security: the threat of physical violence executed by the state and crime organisations, or within the family, and of violence in the workplace and industrial and traffic accidents.

6 Community security: the threat of ethnic tensions and violent clashes.

7 Political security: the threat of human rights violations and state repression.

What happened to this new concept of human security after its launch by the UNDP in 1994?

Human security within policy circles

In the same Human Development Report that introduces the concept of human security, the UNDP demands actual policy responses to tackle the discouraging profile of human insecurity world wide. It is stated that the "edifice of global security built up by humankind" (1994: 35) over the past five decades – in the form of strategic alliances and security pacts – needs change. In its place a new, more encompassing structure must be raised "to ensure the security of all people the world over" (1994: 38). As much as these statements are common place and vague, the awareness that can be deducted from them – that the past overriding emphasis on political security between nation states has often had the effect of lacking attention to the actual *people* belonging to these states and living their daily lives – sounds promising. It is analogue to the awareness of a few years earlier with regard to the socio-economics of development issues. In 1990 The concept of 'human development' and the 'Human Development Index' (HDI) were introduced as it was realised that the macro-economic policy instruments of the 1980s had in many cases contributed to the balancing of national budgets, but that just as often this had been "at the cost of unbalancing people's lives" (UNDP 1995: 117). The idea of putting people at the centre of both human development and human security seems to me laudable common sense – the question remains, however, what *action* can and will be taken in order to effectuate this idea. It is here that three points of criticism must be put forward with regard to the UNDP's concept of human security.

Firstly, if the concept of human security is to be used as a policy concept, even if divided into seven categories, it is too vague a notion to serve as an actual goal to work for by national and international communities and/or agencies. If the UNDP takes its own launching of the concept seriously, it should be more explicit as to which insecurities will be dealt with, why, by whom, and how. The paragraphs on 'early warning indicators' and 'policies for social integration' are phrased in general and sometimes loose terms, and especially so is the idealistic wish to "call on people to make their full contribution to global human security and to bind together in solidarity" (1994: 39). What policy programme will the UNDP write to attain and secure this utopia? Despite the fact that I am not an advocate of the many measuring methods, scales and indexes used by the UNDP, I do think that *only* when the concept is operationalised, some real improvements in people's security positions may be achieved. Unfortunately, of the four subsequent Human Development Reports which each had their own focus none explicitly refers back to the concept of human security – let alone that appropriate indicators have been developed. Then how, I wonder, is this concept going to 'revolutionize' society in the 21st century?

Secondly, the more fundamental question should be raised whether it is at all possible to talk of human security as if it were an objectively measurable quality. Nowhere in the 1994 Human Development Report do I find the observation that the presence or absence of security is mainly a subjective experience of the people involved. Moreover, as Mushakoji rightfully puts forward, different communities often have different systems of belief concerning the relation between human nature and security and these should be taken into account (e.g. Van Dijk & de Bruijn 1995). He furthermore argues that a broader definition of human nature is required, "...not simply rational and selfish as the [Euro-specific] National/International Security assumes, but complex and full of contradictory tendencies. To adopt a Human Security approach implies a total grasp of human nature as it determines the human perception of security and insecurity, threat and reaction to threat. Human security has further to understand the cultural and historical context within which human nature manifests itself, and cease to assume that it is universal" (1994: 44). Mushakoji's critique can be taken to implicitly refer back to what was said about the heterogeneity and fluidity of human experiences and perceptions in the previous chapter on gender.

Lastly, one more essential criticism put forward by Mushakoji is worth stressing at this point. He questions whether the UN, *itself being a western, inter-state institution,* can at all be the judge, guarantor and/or implementor of human security in its new and more encompassing definition (1994: 50; italics mine). After all, 'security' is commonly thought of within the discourse on national and international security which itself is embedded in the modern Western history of nation states. Approaching security problems in regions with a history and culture different from this nation-state security model may *add* to these problems instead of contribute to their solution.

Human security within academic circles

To my knowledge only two academic publications have been explicitly devoted to the subject of human security since the introduction of the concept by the UNDP.[8] Both have their own explicit focus.

First is the substantial publication *Globalization, Competitiveness and Human Security*, edited by Christóbal Kay (1997), a compilation of articles based on papers given at the EADI conference 1996 with the same title. The first article by Helen O'Neill provides the introduction to the theme, where she discusses the different definitions and meanings given to the concepts of globalisation, competitiveness and human security by different authors and 'schools of thought'. As for the concept of human security, she draws exclusively on the UNDP report discussed above and does not argue for amendments or changes in its content. She does remark, however, that "Owing to the widespread concern today with various aspects of human insecurity, it would be appropriate for the UNDP to return to this concept and [...] attempt to provide some measurable indicators relating to it...", and suggests the creation of a 'human security index' to be incorporated into the wider set of development-related indicators (1997: 10). She proceeds by discussing the multifarious relationships between the three core concepts as actual processes characterising today's world, and poses as central the issue whether, and to what extent, globalisation, competitiveness and human security are a positive-sum process. In answering she draws on the so called 'negative school', which highlights the 'winner-take-all' situation in which the Triad of Europe, North-America and Japan benefits disproportionately from (economic) globalisation at the expense of great human economic

---

8 Saying this is not to deny several substantial publications that, more indirectly, cover part of the research area of human security. The most important example is the publication by Von Benda-Beckmann and Marks (eds) (1994) Coping with insecurity: an 'underall' perspective on social security in the Third World. *Special Issue Focaal 22/23*. Several articles from this publication have been included in the annotated bibliography of Part Two. Under a different subject name, Amartya Sen has done much theoretical groundwork for the study of social/human security (e.g. Sen 1981; Ahmad, Drèze, Hills and Sen (eds) 1991).

and social costs borne by the peripheral developing countries. A true 'positive school' attitude is not articulated. O'Neills article deals with human security on a rather abstract level, referring mainly to global economic processes and their consequences for economic marginalisation and insecurity on country (or regional) level. Little mention is made of social consequences for countries or people involved, and the issue of violent (ethnic) conflict is left out altogether. I find this a surprising narrowing of the subject, especially because O'Neill starts her article by explicitly posing the question of how things 'out there' affect people 'in here' – that of globality versus proximity – as central to the whole debate. The next five articles of this publication remain largely on the same level of analysis, and the concept of human security remains either in the background or is dealt with in rather abstract, 'global' terms.

This is by no means to deny that the thorough and lengthy discussion about the effects of globalisation and competitiveness on human security world wide provided in this publication, is very timely and needed. In particular, by connecting the concepts of globalisation and human security, this publication tackles the issue stressed by the UNDP with regard to all its seven types of insecurity delineated, i.e. their *indivisibility* in the current global world. Phrased by the UNDP, "Famine, disease, pollution, drug trafficking, terrorism, ethnic disputes and social disintegration are no longer isolated events, confined within national borders. Their consequences [in terms of human security] travel the globe" (1994: 22). Though I would never question the validity of this statement, in my opinion its flip-side needs to be stressed as well, namely that some security threats disrupting the lives of many people remain conspicuously *local.* I think of the terror that has been spread for more than ten years within the northern districts of Uganda by the Lord's Resistance Army (LRA). The killings and abductions of children are limited to a relatively small area, and 'the world' – despite being very well informed – does not take any action to stop the senseless violence. In other words, I believe that the unprecedented opportunities for genuine transnational or global responsibility (and security) that we have at hand, are being used rather selectively by those nations or regional blocs that happen to be the powerful actors in global affairs today.

The final four articles in *Globalization, Competitiveness and Human Security* (1997) are case studies, and a real treat to those interested in the actual relationships between global and local processes and their effect on people's security as seen and interpreted by the communities involved. These studies convincingly and reassuringly show that "local actors do matter" – one of the assumptions taken as a starting point for this bibliography. In his study of several squatter areas in Manila, Berner (1997), while confirming the viewpoint that globalisation has led to the immediate and physical juxtaposition of global and local, rich and poor, stresses that "the emergence of local territories is not merely a process occurring at the 'underside' of globalisation but a specific counterplay which alters the shape of the world city [...] A locality must be seen as a response to, and an attempt to cope with, the metropolitan environment in the course of a globalisation process which has changed the players and altered the arena" (1997: 179). The security issue that affects the so-called urban poor in Manila most, is that of access to land. Berner discusses the sometimes unexpected sources of power that these urban poor manage to employ against 'global players' through organisation in local associations based on social networks and solidarity. The article by Fiona Wilson (1997) comes closest to the field of interest of this bibliography as it deals with displaced persons in the Peruvian highlands, and the acts of recuperation and reconstruction in which the displaced peasantry, local leaders and government officials find themselves enmeshed in the aftermath of the war waged by 'the Shining Path'. It addresses the issue of human security in the broad sense of material, cultural, social and symbolic reconstruction – a politicised process in which the meanings, intentions, interests and actions of different social actors are at stake.

The second publication dealing with human security is the resource guide *Gender and social security in Central and Eastern Europe and the countries of the former Soviet Union* (Holzner 1997). In their jointly written introduction, Holzner and Truong mention the late 19th century Bismarckian origin of the concept of 'social security' as embedded in the relation between labour and production. With time, the authors state, it was gradually acknowledged that struggles over social security were no longer restricted to the workplace, and therefore new definitions emerged that connected social security issues not only with employment but also with citizenship. From here the authors continue with what they themselves see as the most suitable definition to tackle issues of (in)security. By doing so, they come up with two points of entry that I take as crucial for the perspective of the publication in hand on Refugees, Gender and Human Security.

Firstly, Holzner and Truong find that even the wider definition of social security that evolved (e.g. ILO (1992)), does not suffice to deal with the multiple issues of insecurity apparent in Central and Eastern European countries and those of the former Soviet Union after the 'Big Bang'. In these countries the sudden and short-term transition from centrally-planned to market-oriented economies has effected large scale and multidimensional disruption of social life. These circumstances – and this is the main point – cannot be looked at effectively without taking into account the meaningful participation by members of society in the process of transforming and rebuilding security. People participate – so Holzner and Truong follow Mushakoji (1994) – not only as citizens of a state, but also as actors in many different local and regional social environments that are somehow separated from formal institutional arrangements, and that differ according to place and time. And it is these very actions – I assume the authors wish to suggest – that are often most directly crucial to people's security and well-being. As the concept of social security focuses more or less exclusively on state-provided security, the authors decide to use the concept of human security instead so as to ensure the inclusion of people as active and meaningful participants in the de- and reconstruction of security in their own communities and nations.

Secondly, Holzner and Truong prefer the concept of human security as it includes the issue of gendered (in)security. The theoretical assumption underlying their work, is that all kinds of security are gendered and that men and women experience the erosion of security differently. By taking people seriously as actors in the transformation processes of security and insecurity, the concept of human security at the same time allows for the inclusion of gender differences in this respect. And similarly important, it allows for critical reflection upon the social structures in a given community or nation that maintain, reinforce or create gender differences of insecurity. One example given is how in the new market-oriented economies of former communist states a changing gender ideology (from sameness to difference) and a changing notion of 'Eros' (from desexualised to sexualised), have the effect of legitimising social practices that reinforce the vulnerability and insecurity of women and youth (for example through birth control regulations, prostitution and rape). On the whole, Holzner and Truong conclude, women have far less control over the transition process than men and their identities increasingly become objectified (1997: 19-21). As will be put forward in the next chapter, the mutual relationship between gender ideology and actual differences in gender insecurity is most crucial also in the analysis of insecurity in refugee situations.

CHAPTER 4

BRINGING TOGETHER THE THREE: REFUGEES, GENDER AND HUMAN SECURITY

Now, after the foregoing introduction to the three core concepts of this bibliography – refugees, gender and human security – I will show how bringing together these three concepts can add valuable and timely insights to the current debates on refugee and returnee issues. This last chapter will be a delineation of what I regard as five focal points when combining the three core concepts, and it is these very five points that have guided the search for literature as laid down in part two of this publication.

Human security as an inclusive concept

In both the academic and the refugee relief discourse, human security appears as a wide or all-inclusive concept. The seven categories of threats to human security enumerated by the UNDP can subsume any kind of insecurity one can possibly think of. Similarly Mushakoji's definition, which is taken as starting point also by Holzner and Truong (1997), encompasses "all types of security which involve human individuals and/ or groups protected or protecting against all kinds of threat found in their human environments" (1994: 40). In general it may be true that wide definitions foster obscurity or confusion. However, I believe that there is one overall advantage to be had when linking human security to refugee/returnee issues.

In the introduction and in chapter one it was argued that debates concerning refugees and returnees are often unjustly limited down to the single aspect of politico-legal issues. This tendency may be counteracted when working and studying within the framework of human security. (In)security will then no longer be reduced to political and socio-economic consequences only, but also include the communal and personal, psychological and emotional (in)securities that people struggle with, and learn to deal with, in situations of uprooting and forced migration. The major importance of such an understanding is, in my opinion, that it clarifies that any rigid separation between the different material and non-material dimensions of insecurity in the lives of refugees is *not* in line with reality. The following example is taken from one of my conversations with a young Sudanese man in Kampala. Before he decided to come and try his luck in Kampala, this man lived in Kiryandongo, one of the settlements in Uganda where refugees are supposed to grow their own crops and be self-sufficient. He explained to me how in times of scarcity – no rain, no crops, no relief aid – the young Sudanese girls go to the towns nearby to 'sell themselves to nationals'. Often they come home pregnant, or carry aids. Unmistakably this reality is one of personal – physical and emotional – insecurity for the girls involved. On top of that it very much affects social relationships within the camps. The elderly worry about collapsing community values, the girls are dishonoured, and the young Sudanese men wonder where they will find 'good wives' to build a family.

Thus, the use of the inclusive concept of human security may help to counteract the tendency in both academic studies and relief operations of placing a one-sided emphasis on the material aspects of the supposed needs of refugees. Often this bias in approach remains even long after the acute life-threatening conditions have been overcome. It must be added, of course, that when working with such an inclusive concept as human security, the researcher must be very clear as to what focus or angle he or she wishes to take, what choices are made during the research process, and why. The research field of human security applies to different disciplines, and therefore opens up possibilities for interdisciplinarity in refugee studies. This can furthermore be of great value in supporting relief operations in so called 'refugee affected areas'. Organisations responsible for relief operations are almost by definition faced with a combination of logistic, economic, environmental, health and psychological problems determining the situation at hand. It follows that all these should be addressed in relation to each other if, with a view to the people involved, a successful dealing with the situation is aimed at. Similarly, a thorough knowledge of the multiplicity and complexity of refugee situations will enhance the current efforts by relief organisations – so much urged for by researchers – to connect strategies for emergency policy to long-term development programmes in areas of crisis (Adelman and Sorenson 1994; Harrell-Bond 1986; Kibreab 1985; Stein 1994). Academic interdisciplinarity ideally means that one's research is *actively* embedded in and connected with other projects and fields of knowledge without losing its own focus or expertise. This should work the same way for researchers using the human security framework. Although it is not feasible, nor desirable, to deal with every single aspect of (in)security in the lives of refugees, the advantage in my opinion is that such a framework requires an active awareness on the part of the researcher that the reality for the people involved is always more diverse, more complex, fuller and deeper than it may appear at first sight.

As for my choices, I believe it is important to appreciate and emphasise the non-material needs of refugees to regain a sense of self and human dignity. This is often phrased in terms of a long-term, flexible, negotiable process of re-constructing one's identity. With respect to refugees it is stressed that this process is affected not only by former identities and present influences from the receiving communities, but also by continuing relations that refugees have with their countries of origin as well as with other exiles in their diaspora (Krulfeld 1992). Sarup's words, "identity is not to do with being but with becoming" (1994: 98) seem particularly fitting. As for the search for literature, I put special effort in finding studies that dealt with all kinds of non-material dimensions of (in)security, including issues of identity, belonging and honour (*see in Part Two: Agger 1994; Al-Rasheed 1993; Boddy 1995; Buijs (ed) 1993; Camino and Krulfeld (eds) 1994; Cole et al. (eds) 1992; Donnelly 1994; Flores-Borquez 1995; Gorashi 1997a; Griffiths 1997; Kibreab 1995; McSpadden and Moussa 1993; Monzel 1993; Moussa 1993; Schrijvers 1997; Spring 1979; van Walsum 1994*).

Refugees as agents

Following Mushakoji (1994) and Holzner and Truong (1997), I think it of utmost importance that the concept of human security clearly provides scope to include in one's research "the meaningful participation in a society by its members as a central practice in achieving ... [social security]" (Holzner 1997: 9). In this way the *people* who experience and (try to) cope with insecurity are taken as the central point of departure and the primary focus of analysis. Attention can thus be directed at the diverse and creative ways in which men and women refugees, returnees and internally displaced persons as social actors – individually or in groups – interpret, manage and transform the conditions of their (in)-securities, as well as at the (changing) cultural constructions that underlie their perception of these. Such an approach may help to counteract the still predominant approach towards refugees – put forward in previous chapters – that pictures them as passive victims and clinging recipients of aid. Zetter (1996) in his article about Mozambican refugees in Malawi, suggests that the majority of the refugees interviewed, survived independently of NGO projects, while in fact these projects tended to increase the dependency of participants without having much overall impact. His is just one of quite a number of studies that suggest that outside help is usually much less crucial for the survival of refugees than their own creativity and coping capacities (Harrell-Bond 1986).

I believe that the depth of 'refugee experiences' can only be fully appreciated by addressing the actual life-world (Lebenswelt) of refugees, their immediate and deep-felt experience of not-being-at-home. Again, this means taking into account not only the losses that people suffer, but also the transformations and changes for the better that they make happen. With that in mind, I have tried to search for literature that focuses on acknowledging and bringing to light the experiences of refugees as seen and voiced by themselves, more often than not showing the extraordinary strength of people faced with the dire circumstances of exile and return (*see in Part Two: Flores-Borquez 1995; Gorashi 1997; Hitchcox 1990; Kibreab 1993; Madzokere 1993; Malkki 1996; Panos 1995; Rapone & Simpsom 1996; Schrijvers 1997; Tran 1993; Zetter 1996*). This is at the same time a message to agencies working in the field of refugee assistance to realise that self-organisation by refugees should be stimulated and acted upon far more than is done in most situations now. Painfully illustrative are the remarks by Ranger (1994) in his closing address to the Harare conference of 1991. He repeats how researchers were challenged during this conference by government and agency representatives because they had privileged 'secondary sources' – i.e. the voices of refugees – at the expense of the 'primary sources', i.e. documents produced by governments.

Refugees and gendered (in)security

It was argued in chapter two that gender issues are to be tackled or at least taken into account in any study on forced migration. It is for that very reason that the concept of human security is a particularly useful one from which to enter the field of refugee studies. Holzner and Truong (1997) argue convincingly that all forms of human (in)security are gendered, even though their manifestations, patterns and degree of intensity may be specific and context dependent (think for example of ethnicity, religion, political and economic conditions). The existence and creation of gender insecurity is largely consequential upon the simple fact that social structures, practices and symbols throughout society are gendered. I will give two examples of how (the experience of) insecurity is gendered in the lives of refugees and returnees.

Firstly, refugee situations have illustrated that men and women do not experience the deterioration of security in the same way. This goes for material as well as non-material dimensions of (in)security. Men appear to have more difficulty with the decline in status they experience in exile, and the consequent loss of honour they feel, than women refugees (McSpadden and Moussa 1993; Schrijvers 1997). As for Eritrean refugees, several studies have shown that in the adverse circumstances of exile, it was the women refugees more than the men who resourcefully developed new ways of creating a bearable living for themselves and their communities (e.g. Bright 1992; Kibreab 1995; McSpadden and Moussa 1993; Moussa 1995). This affected existing social security mechanisms and induced new strategies to develop. In Khartoum, for example, Eritrean women set up community restaurants that offered support structures and had the function of information networks among the exiled. Many other women took up work as domestic servants whereas others were compelled to go into prostitution in order to generate sufficient income for the survival of their families. Before their flight to Sudan, the majority of these women had never participated in work outside the home (Kibreab 1995). These developments are all the more interesting in view of the fact that the Eritrean women had to operate in a Sudanese culture where gender relationships and constructs are defined by Islamic law (Kibreab 1995; McSpadden and Moussa 1993).

A second example in fact highlights the opposite. Women refugees are faced with a much more destructive kind of vulnerability than men when it comes to physical insecurity in terms of sexual violence. The sexual violence with which refugee women are confronted, usually takes place against a background of war and persecution – a situation in which daily life is no longer 'ruled' by normal social and moral conventions, and where consequently almost everything is subject to a frightening arbitrariness, which, moreover, often seems to be taken for granted. In passing their verdict on a group of refugee women in 1990 the Dutch High Court trivialised what had happened to these women by bluntly stating that "rape is an expression of the normal sexual drive of the male in times of war" (ter Harmsel 1995: 15). Such an attitude will certainly not help to reveal the frequency of occurrence of sexual violence and the severity of its impact on those refugees who experience it. It is therefore crucial that the advocacy in favour of including gender oppression as a criterion for refugee status is widely and actively supported by researchers (*see in Part Two: Bhabha 1996; Greatbach 1989; Indra 1989; Kathina 1996; Kelly 1994; Mahmud 1996; Oloka-Onyango 1996; Spijkerboer 1994; Zlotnik 1990*). I would like to add that, while being raped or otherwise sexually molested is primarily a personal/individual experience, it also affects the victim's family and community, and thus the wider reality and experience of human security. Women's physical and social vulnerability can be intentionally misused to humiliate their community – as such being used as a war strategy – and at the same time it affects family dynamics by perverting the meaning of intimate relationships (Blackwell 1993). Several authors emphasise that interpersonal relationships are complicated by the taboo that surrounds the topic of sexuality (and especially of sexual violence) in many of the countries that refugees come from. Women often have to cope with strong and confusing feelings of guilt and shame, tied up with the question of complicity. In that situation, non-expression of what has happened can be part of a survival-strategy, so as to avoid social stigmatisation, or worse, the complete rejection by one's partner or community (Agger 1989; Bracken et al. 1995; ter Harmsel 1995). Lastly, it does not have to get to the stage of sexual violence for women to experience gendered insecurity. Bad conditions for giving birth was one of the prominent examples that women refugees from the former Zaire used to give me when I asked them about their worries or insecurities. They said many women died this way.

Gender insecurity, being part and parcel of the daily life experiences of refugees, may never be disregarded in research nor in relief practices. Unfortunately, however – despite often promising rhetoric in documents – gender-blindness in the practice of refugee-aid is on-going and the model of 'the refugee' as an adult male still too often feeds policies. The specific situations of women (and children) therefore do not get the necessary and deserved recognition and attention. Because human security, as argued above, leaves room to take into account individuals as social actors, it simultaneously offers a significant opportunity to address practical gender issues more adequately. This is to be one of the focal points in academic studies of refugees, and a crucial arena for communication between researchers, policy makers and practitioners (*see in Part Two: Cervenak 1994; Cha and Small 1994; Daley 1991; Dzimbiri 1995; Hitchcox 1990; Khasiani 1990; Kibreab 1993; Madzokere 1993; Palmer 1998; Schrijvers 1998; Voutira et al. 1995; Williams 1990; Zetter 1996*).

Global and local (in)securities

In chapter one it was put forward that 'the refugee crisis' pertains to both global and local processes and practices, and that these two cannot be separated when trying to obtain a truthful picture of what is at stake. In the idiom of social security studies, many of the processes that take place in the lives of refugees, returnees and internally displaced persons could well be characterised as issues of 'inclusion and exclusion' on the national and transnational level – an area of study that deserves in-depth research. In the field of international relations a lot of work on this has already been done, linking issues of population movement, population control and (inter)national security. The most important overall lesson that can be learned from such studies, I think, is that refugee movements are political phenomena and thus tied up with regional and international dimensions of power. This reality is sometimes neglected by those partaking in the development discourse on refugees as well as by psychologists and psychiatrists working on refugee trauma. Critics argue that the latter, when diagnosing a refugee as suffering from Post Traumatic Stress Syndrome, thereby pathologise a normal psychological process, which in turn may obscure the fact that "the symptoms of PTSD are not [...] a disorder of the individual, but a natural and lawful response to an intolerable environment" (Ager 1993: 25). Instead of using my own words in order to repeat the argument I made in chapter one for linking global and local studies of (in)security, I will quote Malkki. She writes: "a critical, anthropological engagement with the questions and topics conventionally groupable under 'international relations' might open up new theoretical spaces for conducting ethnographic research on the social imagination of war, peace, and 'world order'; on the use of civilian population displacements in political struggles among states; on the global social life of the arms trade, on the interpenetrations of the language of diplomacy with the language of international refugee aid, and so on" (1995: 505).

The concept of human security is useful because it can be applied to both global issues of exclusion and insecurity and local particularities, as well as to the mutual linkages between these. Apart from the very few articles mentioned in chapter one, studies that actually combine the two are, to my knowledge, still to be designed and carried out. Similarly, very few studies so far have focused on actual local conditions of (in)security and the multiple ways in which these are perceived and coped with by the people themselves (Hirtz 1994; Midgley 1994). The importance of this approach, however, is elaborated by Mushakoji where he states that people's security is crucially different from national security. The nation state as we know it, he writes, is "ready to protect its citizens provided that they do not question its legitimacy." (1994: 46). Ethnic minorities, indigenous people, migrants and also refugees are groups that may not want to give up their identity and may as such choose against integration or identification with the nation state and its nationals. Or else, their integration may be resisted. The consequence, directly or indirectly, often is that these groups do not enjoy the protection of the state and are therefore left with a complex of insecurities, both material and non-material.

Human security and change

The fifth and so far last reason why I think the concept of human security is a very useful one in refugee studies, is because it is particularly applicable in contexts of transition and change. In other words, human security can be applied as a dynamic concept which allows for the study of how past, present and future are tied together in people's perception of (in)security and in the strategies they develop and employ to cope with actual instances of insecurity (see also K. and F. von Benda-Beckmann 1994). Such an approach is indispensable when studying for example the restructuring and renegotiating of security networks that tends to take place in refugee situations. Coming back once more to the situation of Eritrean refugees in Sudan, it is reported that community cohesion has to a large extent broken down, and that market relationships have replaced the main features of the once prevailing social relations between households, which included reciprocal exchanges of food, shelter and labour. Social networks that used to provide support in times of crises weakened, but new ones are being developed, as is clear from the earlier example of community restaurants run by Eritrean women. The effects – both positive and negative – of such changes can only be appreciated in time.

Kibreab states that "A study on refugees is essentially a study on social changes" (1996: 59), and in agreeing with him I believe a dynamic approach to the subject of forced migration is essential. Moreover, it is argued that the study of the multiple processes of change, adjustment and transformation that refugees go through and act upon, may provide new insights for our understanding of processes of culture change in general (Harrell-Bond 1988; Harrell-Bond and Voutira 1992). Another two significant points should receive attention.

Firstly, the changes taking place in the lives of refugees and returnees should not be seen as definite and isolated events. Reestablishment and rehabilitation for example are just names for one phase in an ongoing process which those involved will most probably experience as continuous rather than as divisible in separate entities of space and time (Allen and Morsink 1994). Similarly, the actual moment of flight is not the first nor the sole indicator of future change and insecurity. In most cases it has already been woven through experiences before flight in a society where daily life is disrupted by political oppression or outright violence (Gorashi 1997; Krulfeld and Camino 1994; Daniel and Knudsen 1995). Secondly, I wish to recall the argument made in chapter one that the changes refugees go through may be less strange or paralysing to them than one is often inclined to assume. Movement and crossing boundaries can be part of a way of life, grounded in a history of survival by means of movement. Adding on to this – and coming back to a line of thought that runs through this whole paper – I wish to suggest that the personal and spatial changes that refugees are faced with, are not only those of loss and pain. New environments create new opportunities that may at certain times compensate for the losses suffered, as well as open up new spaces for refugees to re-negotiate former cultural and personal thoughts, values, practices and expectations and create something new.

Literature

Adelman, Howard & John Sorenson (eds) (1994) *African refugees: development aid and repatriation.* Boulder: Westview Press.

Ager, A. (1993) *Mental health issues in refugee populations: a review.* Working paper of the Harvard Center for the Study of Culture and Medicine.

Agger, I. (1989) Sexual torture of political prisoners: an overview. *Journal of Traumatic Stress,* 2 (3): 305-318.

Ahmad, E., J. Dreze, J. Hills & A. Sen (1991) *Social security in developing countries.* Oxford: Clarendon Press.

Allen, Tim & Hubert Morsink (eds) (1994) *When refugees go home.* London: James Currey.

Allen, Tim & Hubert Morsink (1994) Introduction: when refugees go home. In T. Allen & H. Morsink (eds) *When refugees go home.* London: James Currey.

Allen, Tim & David Turton (1996) Introduction. In T. Allen (ed) *In search of cool ground: war, flight and homecoming in Northeast Africa.* London: James Currey.

Allen, Tim (ed) (1996) *In search of cool ground: war, flight and homecoming in Northeast Africa.* London: James Currey.

Appadurai, A. (1990) Disjuncture and difference in the global cultural economy. In M. Featherstone (ed) *Global culture: nationalism, globalization and modernity.* London: Sage Publications.

Bascom, Jonathan (1996) Reconstituting households & reconstructing home areas: the case of returning Eritreans. In T. Allen (ed) *In search of cool ground: war, flight and homecoming in Northeast Africa.* London: James Currey.

Benda-Beckmann, F. and K. von & H. Marks (eds) (1994) *Coping with insecurity: an 'underall' perspective on social security in the Third World.* Special Issue Focaal 22/23.

Berner, Erhard (1997) Opportunities and insecurities: globalisation, localities and the struggle for urban land in Manila. In C. Kay (ed) *Globalisation, competitiveness and human security.* London: Frank Cass.

Blackwell, R. (1993) Disruption and reconstruction of family, network, and community systems following torture, organized violence and exile. In J. Wilson & B. Raphael (eds) *International handbook of traumatic stress syndromes.* New York: Plenum Publishers.

Bracken, P. et al. (1995) Psychological responses to war and atrocity: the limitations of current concepts. *Social Science and Medicine,* 40 (8): 1073-1082.

Braidotti, Rosi (1994) Theories of gender, or: language is a virus. In *Nomadic subjects.* New York: Columbia University Press.

Brandt, E. (1996) Agressie, cultuur en verschrikking: thematiseringen van geweld in antropologisch onderzoek. *Focaal,* 28: 117-125.

Bright, Nancee O. (1992) *Mothers of steel: the women of Um Gargur, an Eritrean settlement in Sudan.* University of Oxford: PhD thesis, Department of Social Anthropology.

Callamard, Agnes (1992) *Refugee assistance, repatriation and development: a gender analysis.* Paper presented at the conference 'First country of asylum and development aid in Malawi', 8-14 June 1992.

Camino, Linda A. & Ruth M. Krulfeld (1994) *Reconstructing lives, recapturing meaning: refugee identity, gender, and culture change.* Washington D.C.: Gordon and Breach Publishers.

Caplan, Pat (1988) Engendering knowledge: the politics of ethnography. *Anthropology Today,* 4 (5): 8-12.

Chanter, Tina (1998) Postmodern subjectivity. In A.M. Jagger & I.M. Young (eds) *A companion to feminist philosophy.* Oxford: Blackwell.

Daniel, Valentine E. & John Knudsen (eds) (1995) *Mistrusting refugees.* Berkeley: University of California Press.

Ferris, Elizabeth (1993) *Beyond borders: refugees, migrants and human rights in the post-cold war era.* Geneva: WCC Publications.

Foucault, Michel (1961) *Madness and civilization: a history of insanity in the age of reason.* London: Routledge.

Foucault, Michel (1972) *The archaeology of knowledge and the discourse on language.* New York: Pantheon.

Girardet, E. (1981) *Somalia keeps its clutches on aid for Ogaden refugees.* Source unknown.

Grant, Judith (1993) *Fundamental feminism: contesting the core concepts of feminist theory.* New York: Routledge.

Habte-Selassie, Elias (1992) Eritrean refugees in the Sudan: a preliminary analysis of voluntary repatriation. In Doornbos et al. (ed) *Beyond conflict in the Horn: prospects for peace, recovery, and development in Ethiopia, Somalia and the Sudan.* London: James Currey.

Haraway, Donna (1991) Situated knowledges: the science question in feminism and the privilege of partial perspective. In D. Haraway (ed) *Symians, cyborgs and women: the reinvention of nature.* New York: Routledge.

Harding, Sandra (1986) *The science question in feminism.* Ithaca/London: Cornell Press.

Harrell-Bond, Barbara E. (1986) *Imposing aid: emergency assistance to refugees.* Oxford/New York/Nairobi: Oxford University Press.

Harrell-Bond, Barbara E. (1988) The sociology of involuntary migration: an introduction. *Current Sociology,* 36 (2): 1-6.

Harrell-Bond, Barbara E. & Ken B. Wilson (1990) Dealing with dying: some anthropological reflections on the need for assistance by refugee relief programmes for bereavement and burial. *Journal of Refugee Studies,* 3 (3).

Harrell-Bond, Barbara E. & Eftihia Voutira (1992) Anthropology and the Study of Refugees. *Anthropology Today,* 8 (4): 6-10.

Harrell-Bond, Barbara E., Eftihia Voutira & Mark Leopold (1992) Counting the refugees: gifts, givers, patrons and clients. *Journal of Refugee Studies,* 5. (3/4).

Harrell-Bond, Barbara E. (1995) *Refugees and the international system: the evolution of solutions.* Oxford RSP: Unpublished paper.

Hirtz, Frank (1994) Issues and authors in the field of social security in the Third World – an introduction. In F. and K. von Benda-Beckmann & H. Marks (eds) *Coping with insecurity: an 'underall' perspective on social security in the Third World.* Special Issue Focaal 22/23.

Holzner, Brigitte (1997) *Gender and social security in Central and Eastern Europe and the countries of the former Soviet Union: a resource guide.* The Hague: ISS/NEDA.

Holzner, Brigitte & Thanh-Dam Truong (1997) Social security versus human security: a gender perspective on problems of transition in Central and Eastern Europe and the countries of the former Soviet Union. In B. Holzner (ed) *Gender and social security in Central and Eastern Europe and the countries of the former Soviet Union.* The Hague: ISS/NEDA.

Horst, Cindy (1998) *A feminist epistemology? Into the field.* Unpublished paper.

ILO (1992) *Social security: a workers' education guide.* Geneva: ILO.

Indra, Doreen M. (1996) Some feminist contributions to refugee studies. In W. Giles, H. Moussa & P. van Esterik (eds) *Development & diaspora: gender and the refugee experience.* Ontario, Canada: Artemis Enterprises.

Kay, Christóbal (ed) (1997) *Globalisation, competitiveness and human security.* London: Frank Cass.

Kibreab, Gaim (1985) *African refugees: reflections on the African refugee problem.* Trenton, N.J.: Africa World.

Kibreab, Gaim (1993) The Myth of Dependency among Camp Refugees in Somalia 1979-1989. *Journal of Refugee Studies,* 6 (4): 321-349.

Kibreab, Gaim (1995) Eritrean Women Refugees in Khartoum, Sudan, 1970-1990. *Journal of Refugee Studies,* 8 (1): 1-25.

Kibreab, Gaim (1996) *Ready and willing... but still waiting: Eritrean refugees in Sudan and the dilemmas of return.* Uppsala, Sweden: Life and Peace Institute.

Kibreab, Gaim (1996) Left in limbo. In T. Allen (ed) *In search of cool ground: war, flight and homecoming in Northeast Africa.* London: James Currey.

Kloos, Peter (1997) *Local identities and global culture.* Paper presented at INDRA lecture series 'Globalisation, Culture and Development: homogenization or a polyphony of voices?', University of Amsterdam.

Kristeva, Julia (1991) *Strangers to ourselves.* Columbia University Press.

Krulfeld, Ruth M. (1992) Cognitive mapping and ethnic identity: the changing concept of community and nationalism in the Laotian diaspora. In P.A. DeVoe (ed) *Selected papers on refugee issues.* Washington, D.C.: American Anthropological Association.

Krulfeld, Ruth M. & Linda A. Camino (1994) Introduction. In L.A. Camino & R.M. Krulfeld (eds) *Reconstructing lives, recapturing meaning: refugee identity, gender, and culture change.* Washington D.C.: Gordon and Breach Publishers.

Kuhlman, Tom (1990) *Burden or boon? A study of Eritrean refugees in the Sudan.* Amsterdam: VU University Press.

Light, Margot (1994) Foreign policy analysis. In A.J.M. Groom & M. Light (eds) *Contemporary international relations: a guide to theory.* London/New York: Pinter Publishers.

Loescher, Gill (1992) Refugee movement and international security. *Adelphi Papers no. 268, IISS,* Brassay's, London.

Loescher, Gill (1993) *Beyond charity: international cooperation and the global refugee crisis.* New York/Oxford: Oxford University Press.

Malkki, Liisa (1992) National Geographic: The Rooting of Peoples and the Territorialization of National Identity among Scholars and Refugees. *Cultural Anthropology,* 7 (1): 24-44.

Malkki, Liisa (1995) Refugees and Exile: From "Refugee Studies" to the National Order of Things. *Annual Review of Anthropology,* 24: 495-523.

McSpadden, Lucia A. & Helene Moussa (1993) I Have a Name: The Gender Dynamics in Asylum and in Resettlement of Ethiopian and Eritrean Refugees in North America. *Journal of Refugee Studies,* 6 (3): 203-225.

Meznaric, Silva (1994) Gender as an ethno-marker: rape, war and identity politics in the former Yugoslavia. In V.M. Moghadam (ed) *Identity politics & women: cultural reassertions and feminisms in international perspective.* Boulder/San Francisco/Oxford: Westview Press.

Midgley, James (1994) Social security policy in developing countries: integrating state and traditional system. In F. and K. von Benda-Beckmann & H. Marks (eds) *Coping with insecurity: an 'underall' perspective on social security in the Third World.* Special Issue Focaal 22/23.

Moghadam, Valentine (1994) *Identity politics and women: cultural reassertions and feminisms in international perspective.* Boulder/Oxford: Westview Press.

Moore, Henrietta (1988) *Feminism and anthropology.* Cambridge: Polity Press.

Moore, Henrietta (1994) *A passion for difference: essays in anthropology and gender.* Cambridge/Oxford: Polity Press.

Moore, Lisa (1993) Among Khmer and Vietnamese refugee women in Thailand: no safe place. In D. Bell, P. Caplan, & W.J. Karim (eds) *Gendered fields: women, men & ethnography.* London: Routledge.

Moussa, Helene (1995) Caught between two worlds: Eritrean women refugees and voluntary repatriation. In Sorenson (ed) *Disaster and development in the Horn of Africa.* UK: Macmillan Press Ltd.

Mushakoji, Kinhide (1994) Human security as an integrative concept for UN policies. *Prime,* 2: 40-52.

Nordstrom, C. & A. Robben (eds) (1995) *Fieldwork under fire. Contemporary studies of violence and survival.* Berkeley/Los Angeles/London: University of California Press.

O'Neill, Helen (1997) Globalisation, competitiveness and human security: challenges for development policy and institutional change. In C. Kay (ed) *Globalisation, competitiveness and human security.* London: Frank Cass.

Papstein, Robert (1991) *Eritrea: revolution at dusk.* New Jersey: The Red Sea Press.

Pateman, Roy (1990) *Even the stones are burning.* New Jersey: The Red Sea Press.

Ranger, Terence (1994) Studying repatriation as part of African social history. In T. Allen & H. Morsink (eds) *When refugees go home.* London: James Currey.

Robertson, Roland (1990) Mapping the global condition: globalization as the central concept. In M. Featherstone (ed) *Global culture: nationalism, globalization and modernity.* London: Sage Publications.

Said, Edward (1990) Reflections on exile. In Schweder (ed) *Out there: marginalisation and contemporary culture.* Cambridge: University Press Cambridge.

Sarup, M. (1994) Home and identity. In Robertson et al. (eds) *Travellers' tales: narratives of home and displacement.* London: Routledge,

Sassen, Saskia (1997) *Losing control? Sovereignty in an age of globalisation.* New York: Columbia University Press.

Schrijvers, Joke (1991) Dialectics of a dialogical ideal: studying down, studying sideways and studying up. In L. Nencel & Pels (eds) *Constructing knowledge: authority and critique in social science.* London: Sage Publications.

Schrijvers, Joke (1997) Internal refugees in Sri Lanka: the interplay of ethnicity and gender. *European Journal of Development Research*, 9 (2): 62-82.

Schrijvers, Joke (1999) Op de vlucht voor idealen? Feministische antropologie onder vuur. *Tijdschrift voor Gender Studies*, 2 (1): 29-39.

Sen, A. (1981) *Poverty and famines: an essay on entitlement and deprivation.* Oxford: Oxford University Press.

Skran, Claudena (1992) The international refugee regime: the historical and contemporary context of international responses to asylum problems. *Journal of Political History*, 4 (1): 8-35.

Stein, Barry (1994) Ad hoc assistance to return movements & long-term development programmes. In T. Allen & H. Morsink (eds) *When refugees go home.* London: James Currey.

Stepputat, Finn (1994) Repatriation and the Politics of Space: The Case of the Mayan Diaspora and Return Movement. *Journal of Refugee Studies*, 7 (2-3): 175-185.

UNDP (1994) *Human Development Report 1994.* Oxford/New York: Oxford University Press.

UNHCR (1997) *The state of the world's refugees.* Geneva: UNHCR.

Van Dijk, Han & Mirjam De Bruijn (1995) *Arid ways: cultural understandings of insecurity in Fulbe society, Central Mali.* Amsterdam: Thela Publications.

Voutira, Eftihia et al. (1995) *Improving social and gender planning in emergency operations.* Oxford: RSP.

Waldron, Sidney (1988) Working in the dark: why social anthropological research is essential in refugee administration, *Journal of Refugee Studies*, 1 (2): 153-165.

Wilson, Fiona (199) Recuperation in the Peruvian Andes. In C. Kay (ed) *Globalisation, competitiveness and human security.* London: Frank Cass.

Zetter, Roger (1991) Labelling refugees: forming and transforming a bureaucratic identity. *Journal of Refugee Studies*, 4 (1): 39-62.

Zetter, Roger (1996) Refugee Survival and NGO Project Assistance: Mozambican Refugees in Malawi. *Community Development Journal*, 31 (3): 214-229.

Zolberg, Aristide R., Astri Suhrke & Sergio Aguayo (1986) International Factors in the Formation of Refugee Movements. *International Migration Review*, 20 (2): 151-169.

Zolberg, Aristide R., Astri Suhrke & Sergio Aguayo (1989) *Escape from violence: conflict and the refugee crisis in the developing world.* New York/Oxford: Oxford University Press.

Part Two

ANNOTATED BIBLIOGRAPHY

Introduction

In the theoretical introduction of Part One, the three concepts central to this publication – refugees, gender and human security – are discussed and placed within the contemporary academic debates on refugee issues. In the last chapter the concepts are taken together and their mutual linkages and importance in relation to each other were put forward. In the same chapter five focal points are delineated that have guided the search for literature as laid down in the following annotated bibliography. These are: human security as an inclusive concept; refugees as agents; refugees and gendered (in)security; global and local (in)securities; and human security and change.

Valuing an active awareness of gender issues in refugee studies as absolutely crucial, 'gender' and 'women' – in relation to forced migration – served as the most important descriptors in this search for literature. It proved impossible to use 'human security' as a descriptor, because the concept does not – with very few exceptions – occur as such in literature. Its subject field has therefore been divided into personal security, health security, political security, legal security, food security and economic security, with relevant descriptors for each category. The fact that in the subject index many references are included in more than just one of these categories, helps to show the indivisibility of people's human security in real life.

As mentioned in Part One, this annotated bibliography focuses on academic articles and books that have been published and are thus available to a wide public. Consequently, very few policy documents and/or evaluation reports by the UNHCR or governments have been included. I wish to draw attention to the extensive bibliography that was compiled only recently, *Women refugees in international perspectives 1980-1990: an annotated bibliography* (Neuwirth & Vincent 1997), which includes a vast number of references to policy documents that deal with gender in terms of the actual needs and problems of particular groups of refugee women in particular regions.

74   REFUGEES, GENDER AND HUMAN SECURITY

Literature to be included in the annotated bibliography, was searched in first instance in two databases with sociological and political science abstracts. Searches were based on relevant descriptors as well as on names of expert authors. In addition, several libraries were used, including the Documentation Centre of the Refugee Studies Programme at Oxford University. The content of the abstracts provided by the International Sociological Association (ISA) in their Sociofile database was, at the explicit request of 'sociological abstracts, inc.', left unaltered, and the copyright is mentioned after every abstract. Inverted commas – " ... " – are used to indicate that the particular abstract is taken from the original text. The remaining abstracts were written by the editor (EL) on the basis of the original texts.

Searches for this annotated bibliography were not limited to a specific time period, and references up to 1999 are included. As such this bibliography updates the existing bibliographies on refugee women (UNHCR 1985, 1989; Neuwirth & Vincent 1997), which cover material written up to 1990 only.

References are presented in alphabetical order by author. A subject index is added, in which the numbers after each keyword refer to the index numbers of the references.

Annotated Bibliography

1   **Adisa, Jinmi (1996)** *The comfort of strangers : the impact of Rwandan refugees on neighbouring countries.* Ibadan: IFRA.
     This volume focuses attention on the impact of the Rwandan refugee exodus on Tanzania and other neighbouring countries, i.e. Uganda, Burundi, and Zaire. The author first discusses the antecedents to the conflict in Rwanda in 1994, and continues with the serious economic, sociopolitical and environmental hardship that the influx of refugees has imposed on the host communities. It is argued that even greater problems are generated by refugee flows back to Rwanda and other neighbouring countries, as these have the potential for destabilizing the whole region. The author suggests a regional approach in order to tackle the multidimensional problem. A distinction is made between short-term requirements (environmental degradation, the issue of compensation, political problems, and gender) and long-term considerations (redrawing the map of national frontiers, refugee villages, resettlement in a third country, repatriation). Finally, the author discusses current efforts, and reviews future needs in order to solve the refugee problem.

2   **Ager, Alastair, Wendy Ager, & Lynellyn Long (1995)** The Differential Experience of Mozambican Refugee Women and Men. *Journal of Refugee Studies,* 8 (3): 265-287.
     "This study examines differences in the experience of Mozambican women and men in refuge in Malawi in late 1990s, with particular regard to the differential impact of assistance policies and programmes. Data collection was through a survey of 420 households and intensive qualitative interviews and daily schedule analysis with a representative focal sample of 20 individual refugees. Samples sites spanned both refugee camps and integrated settlement patterns. Data on educational activity indicated that establish gender inequalities in schooling were perpetuated in the refugee setting. Programmed vocational training activities had little impact on income gen-

eration for either men or women. Whilst incomes were generally very low, the median income for women was zero. Work burden was generally heavier on women. Whilst the health status of men and women was similar, there was evidence of poorer health in female-headed households. Discussion focuses on the inter-relationship between these findings and refugee assistance efforts at the time of the study. In general terms, such assistance had clearly failed to significantly impact the key targets of substantive income generation for women and reduction in female work burden. Indeed, food relief policy and structures for refugee representation appeared to frequently exacerbate gender inequalities. Such findings regarding the differential experience of refugee women and men may be of considerable relevance to the planning and management of future refugee assistance programmes. In particular, the goals of increasing time availability for women and increasing support for indigenous action are commended."

3   **Agger, Inger, & Soren B. Jensen** (1989) Trauma, Meeting and Meaning: Significant Concepts in Transcultural Psychotherapy for Political Refugees; Traume, mode og mening: centrale begreber i transkulturel psykoterapi for politiske flygtninge. *Nordisk Psykologi,* 41 (3): 177-192.
Western clinicians dealing with political refugees are confronted with the trauma of torture as a form of organized crime. Traumatic stress theory provides a context for understanding the symptoms of trauma (panic, anxiety, & deep shame) & principles of posttraumatic therapy can be employed in treatment. Western clinicians have explained their personal counter-transference reactions to the refugees' trauma & social & political problems using the concept of cultural differences. However, this may lead to a new form of racism based on cultural differences. Clinicians & institutions may also experience a secondary traumatization in assisting torture victims. The process of deprivation & reframing of the traumatic torture experiences raises the problem of meaning. In giving testimony, the refugee may be seen as engaging in a meaningful ritual that also gives evidence against the system of repression. 3 Tables, 42 References. Modified AA (Copyright 1990, Sociological Abstracts, Inc., all rights reserved.)

4   **Agger, Inger** (1994) *The blue room: trauma and testimony among refugee women.* London and New Jersey: Zed Books Ltd.
Based on interviews with more than 40 refugee women from the Middle East and Latin America, the book pioneers a new way of understanding and treating women survivors of prolonged trauma. The book is structured

ANNOTATED BIBLIOGRAPHY

around metaphors of rooms and borders that represent women's life experiences from girlhood to womanhood, and their traumas of imprisonment, torture and rape. The author shows how women who are seen to be politically dangerous are punished and controlled, and how this punishment is related to sexual and political power, to culturally transmitted definitions of shame and impurity, and to the seeming paradox of complicity.

5   **Al-Rasheed, Madawi** (1992) Political Migration and Downward Socio-Economic Mobility: The Iraqi Community in London. *New Community,* 18 (4): 537-549.

The history of Iraqi settlement in London, England, is chronicled, showing how successive political events in Iraq have led to the formation of a migrant community over the past forty years. As political migrants who have left home under various pressures, the Iraqi experience of migration is in many ways different from the classical economic migration. The relationship between political migration & the trend toward downward socioeconomic mobility among a subsection of the migrant community is discussed, drawing on data obtained 1990/91 via interviews & questionnaires from a sample of 150 Iraqis in London. Focus is on the internal constraints & obstacles imposed by the host society that maintain the decline in the community's standard of living. 22 References. Adapted from the source document. (Copyright 1993, Sociological Abstracts, Inc., all rights reserved.)

6   **Al-Rasheed, Madawi** (1993) The Meaning of Marriage and Status in Exile: The Experience of Iraqi Women. *Journal of Refugee Studies,* 6 (2): 89-104.

"This paper focuses on the experience of women who become exiles as a result of the decisions and political involvement of their husbands. The experience of exiled Iraqi women in London is examined. Exile in their case precipitates a state of liminality and a crisis of meaning experienced at the level of marriage and family life. It is argued that in exile, women reconstruct images of marriage which they associate with status and security, the two aspects which their marriages lack when they become refugees."

7   **Al-Rasheed, Madawi** (1994) The Myth of Return: Iraqi Arab and Assyrian Refugees in London. *Journal of Refugee Studies,* 7 (2-3): 199-219.

"Drawing on the theoretical development in the field of migration studies, this paper examines the relevance of the 'myth of return' to refugee groups. It rejects the assumption that refugees' attachment to their homeland and their desire to return to it are 'natural' givens. The myth of return and its predominance among a refugee community are dependent on past refugee experiences and the relationship of the group with its country of origin. This is illustrated by considering two cases of refugee groups: Iraqi Arabs and Iraqi Assyrians. The first belong to the mainstream population of the country, whereas the second are a Christian minority in Iraq. The paper concludes that the presence or absence of the myth of return among refugee groups is important for understanding not only the relationship with the homeland, but also the relationship with the host country."

✦ 8   **Allen, Tim, & Hubert Morsink (eds)** (1994) *When refugees go home.* London: James Currey.

This is a collection of papers that arose from the Harare conference on the socio-economic aspects of repatriation, organised by UNRISD (1991) as part of its research programme on 'Refugees, returnees and local society'. Most papers are based on detailed case studies of returned populations in Africa, and tackle issues concerning the (lack of) international assistance to returnees. Also the alleged 'dependency syndrome' of refugees is addressed in many of the papers. This book is the first extensive publication on the issue of repatriation and as such it contributes to filling an important research gap. Separate chapters by Rogge, Stein, Bouhouche, Akol, Kabera & Muyanja, Makanya, Jackson, Wilson&Nunes, Wilson, Papscott, Preston, Arhin, van Haer and Ranger (some of which are included in this annotated bibliography).

9   **Allen, Tim (ed)** (1996) *In search of cool ground: war, flight and home-coming in Northeast Africa.* London: James Currey.

This second collection of papers on the subject of repatriation in (Northeast) Africa arose from the Addis Abeba conference (1992), organised by UNRISD as part of its research programme on 'Refugees, returnees and local society'. The book is intended as a companion volume to Allen & Morsink (eds) 1994, taking arguments a stage further. Separate chapters by Opondo, Hendrie, Habte-Selassie, Kibreab, Bascom, Styan, Turton, Getachew, Farah, Holt, Hogg, Mohamed Salih, Johnson, James, Brett, Allen, Parker, Endale, Brett, Cernea and Ranger (some of which are included in this annotated bibliography).

ANNOTATED BIBLIOGRAPHY

79

10 **Aptekar, Lewis, Brechtje Paardekooper, & Janet Kuebli** (1999) Adolescence and youth among displaced Ethiopians: a case study in Kaliti Camp. *World Psychology,* Special edition on Adolescence, in press.

The effects of trauma on adolescent mental health were studied via ethnographic fieldwork and the application of psychological testing. A random sampling of 108 war-traumatized subjects (86 male and 40 female) was given the Trauma Event subscale of the Harvard Trauma Questionnaire and the Symptom Checklist 90-Revised. More than 90% of the sample lost their property, 70% suffered extreme thirst, and more than third witnessed death. They had all been living for the past six years in an extremely poor camp for the displaced. Yet, the psycho pathology of the group was considerably less than expected. The authors attributed this to the adolescents' appraisal of the particular circumstances of their lives. They compared their poverty with other Ethiopians, and they compared their relative freedom given to them by their community with adolescence of their parents and of other Ethiopians. The openness of the community in allowing adolescents to live outside of traditional norms was particularly salient for the females. The authors concluded that situation and circumstantial factors must be considered in assessing the mental health of war-traumatized adolescents.

11 **Ardener, Shirley, & Sandra Burman (eds)** (1995) *Money-go-rounds: the importance of rotating savings and credit associations for women.* Oxford: Berg Publishers.

This book reviews the role of Rotating Saving and Credit Associations (ROSCAS) in Africa and Asia as well as among diaspora communities in Europe, the USA and the Carribean. The idea of the ROSCAS is that they allow women to make regular savings that are controlled by them and are based on trust and peer pressure. The operation of ROSCAS among refugee and other migrant communities has long been neglected. In this book six chapters deal with such situations, two with regard to refugee women and four regarding migrant communities. As regards refugees, Almedon compares the role of ROSCAS among Ethiopian women in Addis Abeba and Eritrean women in Oxford, while Summerfield deals with the *Hagbad* in both Somalia and the UK. Both chapters show how the rosca institutions provide important sources of finance as well as social and support networks for women living in exile.

12 **Bankston, Carl L.** (1995) Gender Roles and Scholastic Performance among Adolescent Vietnamese Women: The Paradox of Ethnic Patriarchy. *Sociological Focus,* 28 (2): 161-176.

The advancing status of Vietnamese-American women, members of an ethnic group with strong patriarchal traditions in the home country, is usually interpreted as a result of the increasing adoption of relatively egalitarian US vs traditional Vietnamese perspectives on sex-appropriate behavior. It is argued here that in one important area of advancement, education, young Vietnamese-American women are actually surpassing the performance of male coethnics, although older Vietnamese women show significantly lower levels of education than men. Interview data obtained in an overseas Vietnamese community designed to prepare refugees for resettlement, & participant observation in a Vietnamese-American community in New Orleans, LA, are drawn on to argue that this educational performance occurs not because of the abandonment of patriarchal views, but rather, ironically, because of the persistence of these views, which place greater social controls on young women than on young men. 6 Tables, 21 References. Adapted from the source document. (Copyright 1996, Sociological Abstracts, Inc., all rights reserved.)

13 **Barsky, Robert** (1994) *Constructing a productive other: discourse theory and the Convention Refugee Hearing.* Amsterdam: Benjamins.

This book brings in discourse theory and textual analysis to bear upon transcripts of refugee applicant hearings in Canada, with the latter being conducted within the legal framework of the United Nations Convention on Refugees. Analytic and sociolinguistic theories by Mikhail Bhaktin, Pierre Bourdieu and Habermas are used by the author for a critical theoretical analysis of the interactions and linguistic exchanges taking place between refugee claimants and immigration officers. Barsky is very critical about the hearing process and concludes that it renders the refugee Other 'un-dialogic' and thus a non-self. He argues for a dialogically open hearing process.

14 **Bascom, Jonathan** (1996) Reconstituting households & reconstructing home areas: the case of returning Eritreans. In T. Allen *In search of cool ground: war, flight and homecoming in Northeast Africa.* London: James Currey.

This article is based on an intensive case study in Wad el Hilau (1987-8, 1992), which forms the largest concentration of unassisted, rural refugees from Eritrea in eastern Sudan. The prospects for repatriation are assessed, with as main focus an investigation into the ways in which repatriation decisions on the part of refugees are linked to their subsequent processes of reintegration. Intra- and inter household dynamics are discussed (including gender issues) as well as the problems Eritrean returnees will be faced with upon return in terms of changed urban and rural expectations. The author shows and argues that active participation by the Eritrean returnees in the process of reconstructing the areas to which they return, is a fundamental prerequisite for the rehabilitation and development of these regions. This conclusion should be taken up in ongoing repatriation programmes.

15 **Baskauskas, Liucija** (1981) The Lithuanian refugee experience and grief. *International Migration Review*, 276-291.
"This article argues that though a population of refugees may experience the process of assimilation / acculturation as well as that of multiple identity formation with ever changing group boundary maintenance mechanisms, they also experience grief, which accounts for a variety of their individual and collective behaviors."

16 **Beaglehole, Ann** (1990) *Facing the past: looking back at refugee childhood in New Zealand 1940s-1960s.* Wellington: Allen & Unwin.
This book explores the experiences of refugees – primarily Jews from Central and Eastern Europe – who came to New Zealand as children or adolescents in the 1930s, 1940s and 1950s, as well as the experiences of New Zealand-born children of refugees. The author makes extensive use of interview material throughout the text. Two themes run through most interviews: first, the consequences of a lack of continuity between past and present, and second issues of identity in the refugee children's experiences of belonging and non-belonging. The author tries to understand refugee childhood as an interactive process set in the contact between the 'new' and the 'old world' , and shows how both the struggle to belong and the choice to remain outsider must be viewed as ambiguous and complex experiences in a particular historical context.

17 **Benard, C.** (1994) Rape as terror: the case of Bosnia. *Terrorism and political violence*, 6 (1): 29-43.
This paper examines the significance of rape as a deliberate instrument of terror in the context of war by using Bosnia since 1992 as a case study. Political science has generally neglected this phenomenon, but has instead generally adhered to the popular view that rape is simply a by-product of war. This

article now seeks to distinguish contexts and functions of rape on the basis of socio-military ideology, intent and consequences, and four distinct configurations of wartime rape are identified (bounty, outlet, breakdown, deliberate strategy). Based on data from 250 interviews with Bosnian refugees in Croatia and Austria, the tactical functions of rape as a part of "ethnic cleansing" are described, and parallels are determined between rape and the terrorizing of other vulnerable civilians such as children. Incidental reports of the efforts of individual dissenting soldiers to prevent rape are also mentioned. It is concluded that while a tactical interpretation of rape is illuminating, it leaves many questions concerning the willingness of large numbers of men to employ sexual violence.

18 **Benson, Janet** (1994) Reinterpreting gender: Southeast Asian refugees in American society. In L.A. Camino & R.M. Krulfeld (eds) *Reconstructing lives, recapturing meaning: refugee identity, gender and culture change.* Washington D.C.: Gordon and Breach Publishers, pp. 75-96.

This article is based on fieldwork (1989-1992) in three southwest Kansas communities that have attracted large numbers of refugees and immigrants to work in the region's meatpacking industry. The article focuses on the process of reinterpreting gender as Southeast Asian refugees in these Kansas communities cope with financial needs, the legal system and American concepts of gender roles. The term 'reinterpreting' is used by the author to suggest both cultural continuity and the need for adaptation in a new environment. She finds that continuity is stronger than change with the first generation of refugees, while the second generation must mediate between two different cultural worlds. Furthermore, the author argues that the Vietnamese and Laotien women have their own power bases within the family, of which some are enhanced through encounters with American society, whereas others are lost in the process of acculturation.

19 **Berner, Erhard** (1997) Opportunities and insecurities: globalisation, localities and the struggle for urban land in Manila. In C. Kay (ed) *Globalisation, competitiveness and human security.* London: Frank Cass, pp. 167-182.

"Globalisation is a contradictory process: integration on a global scale is connected to processes of fragmentation within world cities. The juxtaposition of global and local, rich and poor, skyscrapers and squatter shacks is characteristic of Manila as of every other metropolis. Based on an empirical study of squatter areas, the research found that everyday life in the locality is the major basis for the emergence of organised groups. Local associations form alliances with NGOs, the support of the media and church, and force politicians and land developers to take their existence into consideration. The paramount goal of squatter organisations is habitat defence and security of tenure. Despite many setbacks, they have made considerable progress in recent years."

20 **Bhabha, Jacqueline** (1993) Legal problems of women refugees. *Women: a cultural review*, 4 (3): 240-249.

In this paper the author examines the problems that refugee women are faced with due to the fact that gender is absent as a ground of persecution in the Refugee Convention. She highlights the gender-blindness of the refugee definition through a discussion of sexual violence ranging from domestic violence to rape in war. She also adds the difficulties experienced by 'women who transgress cultural norms'. The author concludes with the example of the international precedents set by the authorities in Canada: the acceptance of refugee women's claims based on persecution by non-governmental persecutors, and the granting of protection to women fearing persecution for transgressing their society's customary norms. The paper is illustrated by case histories.

21 **Bhabha, Jacqueline** (1996) Embodied Rights: Gender Persecution, State Sovereignty, and Refugees. *Public Culture,* 9 (1): 3-32.

As the number of refugees escalates & the commitment to refugee protection in the West is superseded by immigration restriction & border fortification, the ethical limitations of the post-Cold War international order are exposed. This is particularly evident in gender persecution cases, where private choices clash with public expectations of gendered identity, revealing unresolved tensions between individual & state interests in relation to the control of sexuality. To make this case, the claims of various female asylum seekers are compared: an Iranian Muslim women fleeing Islamic norms, a Jordanian Muslim woman fleeing domestic violence, several Chinese women fleeing their country's population control program, & several African women fleeing female genital mutilation. The US court decisions in the Muslim cases would seem to reflect a gradual but growing judicial acceptance of gender persecution as a valid ground for the granting of refugee status, but the decisions in the Chinese & African cases suggest that there is a double standard as well. M. Maguire (Copyright 1997, Sociological Abstracts, Inc., all rights reserved.)

22 **Bissland, Julie, & Landgren, Karin (eds)** (1997) International Journal of Refugee Law, Special Issue on gender-based persecution. *International Journal of Refugee Law.*

This special issue is based on the UNHCR Symposium on Gender-based Persecution, held in Geneva on 22-23 February 1996. It is divided into the following parts: opening statements; report of the symposium; country presentations; gender related refugee claims; the need for guidelines, and their formulation and use to date.

23 **Black, Richard** (1994) Livelihoods under stress: a case study of refugee vulnerability in Greece. *Journal of Refugee Studies,* 7 (4): 360-377.

"The paper examines the concept of 'vulnerability' drawing on literature on welfare systems in the developed world, and vulnerability to famine and disasters in the Third World. The concept is applied to a case study of refugee vulnerability in Greece. Factors influencing the livelihood and vulnerability of a sample of refugee households and individuals living in Athens 1992 are considered. It is argued that vulnerability must be viewed in terms not only of the characteristics of individuals and households, but also in terms of the context of state policies and the wider characteristics of society and the economy. A number of elements both of Greek policy and society that significantly increase refugee vulnerability are identified, along with actual and potential responses of agencies providing assistance to refugees."

24 **Blakeney, Jill, Fadumo J. Dirie, & Mary A. MacRae** (1996) Support group for traumatized Somali women: a pilot project of the Canadian Centre for Victims of Torture. In W. Giles, H. Moussa, & P. v. Esterik (eds) *Development and diaspora: gender and the refugee experience.* Canada: Artemis Enterprises, pp. 280-301.

"The authors of this paper examine how somali women have challenged identity politics in their everyday lives. In the support group organized for Somali women, one of the key group dynamics that emerged was the absence of inter-clan animosity. The common problems the women faced as women, as wives and mothers, as newcomers to Canada, and as torture victims transcended any clan divisions. Other differences such as age, education, and rural-urban backgrounds, or degree of Islamic religious orthodoxy not only did not hinder group solidarity but are described as having enriched and enlivened discussion."

Annotated Bibliography

25 **Boddy, Janice** (1995) Managing tradition: 'Superstition' and the making of national identity among Sudanese women refugees. In W. James (ed) *The pursuit of certainty: religious and cultural formulations.* London/New York: Routledge, pp. 15-44.

Drawing on 1991/92 ethnographic fieldwork, this paper investigates the efforts by Sudanese female immigrants and refugees in Toronto, Ontario, to develop a strong sense of cultural identity through participation in a *zar* (spirit possession ritual) and a traditional Sudanese wedding. In the zar, women both challenge and express the embodied knowledge of their roles in local communities. It is noted that religious elements of the zar have been outlawed by the government in Sudan in its quest to gain absolute control over culture and women. As practiced in combination with the traditional Sudanese wedding, it is suggested that the zar represents a staged collision of certainties, givens, and absolutes that weave together traditional cultural elements in the manner of bricolage. As such these practices represent resistance to social convention and masculine authority, which are experienced by the women in traditional Sudanese culture, through foreign oppression and through xenophobia.

26 **Bolzman, Claudio, & Rosita Fibbi** (1991) Collective Assertion Strategies of Immigrants in Switzerland. *International Sociology*, 6 (3): 321-341.

It is argued that changes in both the political & cultural collective assertion strategies of immigrants in Switzerland are due to the immigrants' experience of status inconsistency, which includes socioeconomic opportunities & excludes political participation. This inequality is a result of Swiss migration policy & the structure of political opportunities. These assertions are tested by a documentary analysis & a survey of 25 immigrant associations in the canton of Geneva. The findings support the hypothesis that a lack of socioeconomic or political rights stimulates social mobilization among immigrant groups, especially at the local community level. It is concluded that whatever the kinds of barriers immigrants face in their confrontation with the host society, their response is to develop certain forms of cultural & political self-assertion in order to better negotiate their status within the host society. 4 Tables, 1 Figure, 33 References. Adapted from the source document. (Copyright 1992, Sociological Abstracts, Inc., all rights reserved.)

27 **Bolzman, Claudio** (1994) Stages and Modes of Incorporation of Exiles in Switzerland: The Example of Chilean Refugees. *Innovation*, 7 (3): 321-333.

Many scholars perceive the incorporation of refugees & immigrants to a new society as a matter of time: the longer the length of residence, the more the refugees & immigrants perceive their stay in the host society as permanent. Here, it is argued that incorporation to a new society is not necessarily a linear process depending exclusively on length of residence, nor is assimilation necessarily the end result of this process. Instead, linear & assimilationist approaches neglect macrosocial context &, to a lesser extent, social stratification, both of which are important variables influencing the incorporation process of migrants to a new society. The example of Chilean refugees in Switzerland shows the relevance of these factors & also of the actor's own perception of the situation in the definition of different stages of exile. 36 References. Adapted from the source document. (Copyright 1995, Sociological Abstracts, Inc., all rights reserved.)

28 **Boone, Margaret S.** (1994) Thirty year retrospective on the adjustment of Cuban refugee women. In L.A. Camino & R.M. Krulfeld (eds) *Reconstructing lives, recapturing meaning: refugee identity, gender and culture change.* Washington D.C.: Gordon and Breach Publishers, pp. 179-201.

This article discusses interviews with five Cuban women living in the Washington D.C. area with the purpose of determining the types of changes these women have undergone during the thirty years after the Cuban revolution (1959). The interviews focus on sex role changes in order to 'tease apart' and explain the nature and strength of Cuban cultural beliefs about appropriate relations between the sexes. The women have changed in ways that are consistent with their cultural heritage and their experiences provide a useful, long-term, temporal perspective on the effects of gender on the adjustment of refugees in American society.

29 **Bracken, Patrick, Joan Giller, & Derek Summerfield** (1997) Rethinking mental health work with survivors of wartime violence and refugees. *Journal of Refugee Studies,* 10 (4): 431-442.

"Of late there has been a proliferation of centres and programmes providing mental health care for refugees and victims of violence. This proliferation has mainly occurred in Western countries, but an increasing number of projects have been delivered to Third World war zones in the name of the treatment of 'war trauma'. Western psychology and psychiatry provide the theoretical and therapeutic tools which are used by most of these projects.

This paper argues that because these tools are not value neutral, there are profound ethical problems associated with this work. The insights developed by a number of post-modern theorists are used to provide as framework for discussing these problems."

30 **Brody, Eugene** (1994) The mental health and well-being of refugees: issues and directions. In A. Marsella et al. (eds) *Amidst peril and pain: the mental health and well-being of the world's refugees.* Washington D.C.: American Psychological Association, pp. 57-80.

"This paper offers an overview of the many mental health problems associated with the refugee experience and the need to approach these problems at national, governmental, and international levels. It highlights the wide-ranging and long-term consequences of the refugee experience."

31 **Brouwer, Roland** (1994) Insecure at home: emigration and social security in northern Portugal. In K. and F. von Benda-Beckmann & H. Marks (eds) *Coping with insecurity: an 'underall' perspective on social security in the Third World.* Special Issue Focaal 22/23, pp. 153-176.

This paper deals with the relationship between migration and the organization of social security and security networks. The author starts with a brief discussion of the migration issue in general, arguing that the concept of migration implies a wide spectrum of population movements. He then focuses attention on the Portuguese situation in the twentieth century, distinguishing three migratory waves. The second part of the paper deals with the effects of emigration on the population that stays behind, in particular with respect to the organization of their social security. Case material is taken from the Vila Real district in northern Portugal.

32 **Bruijn, Mirjam de** (1994) The Sahelian crisis and the poor: the role of Islam in social security among Fulbe pastoralists, central Mali. In K. and F. von Benda-Beckmann & H. Marks (eds) *Coping with insecurity: an 'underall' perspective on social security in the Third World.* Special Issue Focaal 22/23, pp. 47-64.

This paper examines how poor members of Fulbe society, a group of agropastoralists in the Sahel, central Mali, are surviving after two decades of environmental disaster. The focus is on the Jalloube of the Hayre in central Mali. Social security relations and institutions based on Islam seem to be becoming more important for these people, who are not sufficiently supported anymore by 'traditional' social security mechanisms. Islam has a long history in the Hayre, as have its institutions such as 'zakat' (the basis of the Islamic principle of charity), Koranic schools and networks of Moodibaabe (Islamic scholars). The harsh circumstances in which the Jalloube live have given new values and importance to these institutions and to social relations based on Islam: new networks based on Islam are being explored; 'zakat' has become much more an institution directed at alleviating poverty and is replacing other obligatory kinship-based gift relations; Islamic knowledge and the status related to it open up new possibilities of survival. Fieldwork for this study was carried out in 1990-1992 in the 'cercle' Douentza.

• 33   **Buijs, Gina (ed)** (1993) *Migrant women: crossing boundaries and changing identities.* Oxford and Providence: Berg Publishers Ltd.

This book deals with the experiences of migrant and refugee women who find themselves in the process of adaptation to new environments and ways of life. Most of the women studied in this volume hoped to retain their original culture and lifestyle at least to some extent, but found that the exigencies of being migrants and refugees forced them to examine their preconceptions and to adopt roles, both social and economic, which they would have rejected at home. On the other hand, for some women emigration also provided a means of achieving a social and economic mobility that they would have been denied at home. Chapters by Buijs, Lund Skar, Eastmond, Abdulrahim, Summerfield, Bhachu, Mascarenhas-Keyes, Hitchcox, Swaisland.

34   **Cagan, Beth, & Steve Cagan** (1991) *This promised land, El Salvador: the refugee community of Colomoncagua and their return to Morazan.* New Brunswick/London: Rutgers University Press.

This book presents an account of the experiences of Salvadorean refugees during exile in Honduras as well as their decision-making process for return and their efforts in rebuilding community life after they have actually returned spontaneously to El Salvador. The refugees' experiences are central to the book in which extensive use is made of direct quotes and of photographs. The authors emphasise the extraordinary strength and survival of these refugees who did not depend on international assistance, as well as their high level of organisation.

35 **Callamard, Agnes** (1994) Refugees and local hosts: a study of the trading interactions between Mozambican refugees and Malawian villagers in the district of Mwanza. *Journal of Refugee Studies,* 7 (1): 39-62.

"Based on empirical data collected in the district of Mwanza, Malawi, this paper explores one particular dimension of the local impact of a refugee camp, namely the development of trading interactions between refugees and hosts, and seeks to identify the structural, policy and individual-based variables that determined the nature and extent of inter-community trade. It especially shows that *a priori* negative structural and policy factors, including shortcomings of the refugees' food basket, diversion of food relief, and a local economy dominated by the subsistence sector, gave rise to a flourishing trading system. Refugees' and hosts' trade accelerated the social stratification process within the camp while resulting in increased commoditization of exchanges at the local level. Refugee men with the longest duration of stay in Malawi, local women and villagers with access to wet land are shown to be primary actors and beneficiaries of the development of the trading system. The potential victims of trading activities were refugee children and refugee women, but no such 'losers' were identified among the villagers."

36 **Callamard, Agnes** (1996) Flour is power: the gendered division of labour in Lisongwe Camp. In W. Giles, H. Moussa, & P.van Esterik (eds) *Development and diaspora: gender and the refugee experience.* Canada: Artemis Enterprises, pp. 176-198.

"This paper – set in a refugee camp for Mozambican refugees in Malawi – discusses how the gendered division of labour is a dynamic rather than a static process, responding to socio-economic transformations. Activities for women are concentrated heavily on reproductive as opposed to productive forms of work. Women's reproductive roles are described as pillars of the camp, but their access to decision-making roles and to control of resources is very limited."

37 **Callaway, Helen** (1987) Women refugees: specific requirements and untapped resources. In G. Altaf (ed) *Third world affairs.* London: Third World Affairs Foundation , pp. 320-325.

In this paper the author argues that in refugee policy and assistance the special needs and vulnerability of refugee women has not been sufficiently considered, nor have their pivotal position in the household economy and their special capacities and strengths been appreciated. She addresses practical issues of refugee women's health, food security and economic self-sufficiency, and more generally argues for a rethinking of the conceptual framework of refugee policy in terms of gender difference.

38   **Caloz-Tschopp, Marie C., & Lindsay Hossack** (1997) On the Detention of Aliens: The Impact on Democratic Rights. *Journal of Refugee Studies,* 10 (2): 165-180.

"Within the context of the sociohistorical framework of globalization, this paper examines how aliens without documents experience democracy in Europe. In order to establish what is at stake, the author examines detention, the threat to human rights and to democracy as a system of government, drawing on empirical evidence as well as philosophical thinking. First the paper identifies the political elements of democracy and how detention – with its attendant deprivation of rights – changes a liberal democracy into a defensive one. The paper then turns to philosophical consideration. It presents an image of society entering a new phase – one of violence engendered by globalization – and challenges us to envisage a reformed political system sensitive to humanitarian needs."

39   **Camino, Linda A.** (1994) Refugee adolescents and their changing identities. In L.A. Camino & R.M. Krulfeld (eds) *Reconstructing lives, recapturing meaning: refugee identity, gender and culture change.* Washington D.C.: Gordon and Breach Publishers, pp. 29-56.

This paper deals with the interrelations between ethnic and refugee identity through a study of a group of refugee and immigrant adolescents from Latin America who resettled in an urban area in the United States. It demonstrates that these youths developed new collective identities that presented themselves systematically depending not only on images/memories of the homeland but also on their present context, and therefore being fluid rather than single or static. Adults in the lives of these refugee adolescents played an important role in facilitating the development of new identities through a community-based 'drop-in center'. The author concludes that the flexible discourse on ethnicity enabled the adolescents to 'try out' different identities, and that this trying out of identities constitutes a crucial component in the adaptation of refugees to their new societies.

ANNOTATED BIBLIOGRAPHY

40 **Camino, Linda A., & Ruth M. Krulfeld (ed)** (1994) *Reconstructing lives, recapturing meaning: refugee identity, gender and culture change.* Washington D.C.: Gordon and Breach Publishers.

This book presents a thorough and elaborate investigation of refugees' loss of their old identities and their efforts to construct new ones. It critically examines the interplay between cultural, ethnic, and gender constructions among resettled refugee populations. Each chapter is grounded in anthropological theory and method, and the book's framework demonstrates the relationship between the dynamics of forced migration and the ways in which ethnic and gender identities are reinvented in new socio-cultural settings. Refugee resettlement is seen as a creative, experimental process. Separate chapters by Benson, Boone, Camino, DeVoe, Earle, Krulfeld, Kulig, Markowitz, Mortland and Omidian are included in this annotated bibliography.

41 **Camus-Jaqcues, Genevieve** (1990) Refugee women: the forgotten majority. In G. Loescher & L. Monahan (eds) *Refugees and international relations.* Oxford: Clarendon Press, pp. 141-157.

Although the majority of the world's refugees are women and girls, very little research or assistance is aimed directly at them. By discussing the variety of issues pertinent to refugee women's protection and assistance problems, the author hopes to offer direction for badly needed new investigation and research. Based on examples, the special problems of refugee women regarding protection, assistance and participation in decision-making are identified, including the newly emerging need to recognize as refugees women who suffer persecution in their own country because of their sexual status. Recommendations are made. (adapted from Neuwirth & Vincent [1997])

42 **Cernea, Michael M.** (1990) Internal refugee flows and development-induced population displacement. *Journal of Refugee Studies,* 3 (4): 320.

"An unjustified dichotomy in the social science literature dealing with displaced populations separates the study of refugees from the study of populations uprooted by development projects. The paper argues that this dichotomy must be overcome by exploring the similarities and differences between these categories of displaced populations. Both bodies of literature, which currently do not 'speak to each other', stand to gain conceptually from overcoming their relative isolation. New trends are signalled regarding the international aid and assistance channeled during the 1980s to refugee and displaced populations. The paper discusses the worldwide growth of development-related population displacements, while in many countries domestic policies and legal frameworks to guide forced dislocation and resettlement are lacking. The differences between relief and development oriented strategies for resettling displaced people are examined with emphasis on the importance of allocating adequate resources for the sustainable socio-economic re-establishment of people displaced by development."

43 **Cernea, Michael M.** (1995) Understanding and preventing impoverishment from displacement: reflections on the state of knowledge. *Journal of Refugee Studies,* 8 (3).

"The remarkable progress in social science research on resettlement during the last decade is defined by the author in terms of (a) knowledge acquisition – the addition of considerable in-depth and 'extensive' new knowledge; (b) significant shifts in research trends – from academic inquiry to operational research, from description to prescription, from writing ethnographies of past cases to crafting forward-looking policy frameworks; and (c) development and diversification of research models – particularly an evolution from the stress-centred model to the impoverishment/re-establishment centred model in analysing resettlement. The impoverishment risks model consists of eight recurrent and interlinked processes. It reveals how multifaceted impoverishment caused by displacement occurs via induced landlessness, joblessness, homelessness, marginalization, increased morbidity, food insecurity, loss of access to common property and social disarticulation. The conceptual model of impoverishment through displacement also contains, in essence, the model for the positive re-establishment of those displaced, which requires turning the impoverishment model on its head. The author analyses in detail the drop and the reversal in the income curve of resettlers during displacement and relocation, and points out the financial premises for income recovery. The two key priorities recommended for future resettlement research are: (a) research on re-establishment experiences, and (b) research on the economics of displacement and recovery."

44 **Cervenak, Christine M.** (1994) Promoting Inequality: Gender-Based Discrimination in UNRWA's Approach to Palestine Refugee Status. *Human Rights Quarterly,* 16 (2): 300-374.

Gender discrimination in the UN Relief & Works Agency for Palestine Refugees (UNRWA) is examined. The UNRWA uses a patrilineal model for determining Palestine refugee status, ie, viewing refugee status as conveyed from generation to generation through the father. Palestine refugee men can marry nonrefugee women & transmit refugee status to their children. However, Palestine refugee women married to nonrefugee men cannot transmit refugee status to their children. This model conflicts with international legal norms & adversely impacts a large portion of the Palestine population by excluding them from UN education, health, & economic assistance. The model likely stems from reliance on existing Palestinian institutions & Arab law. Alternative approaches to gender & generational issues of legal identity are discussed. D. Generoli (Copyright 1995, Sociological Abstracts, Inc., all rights reserved.)

45 **Cha, Dia, & Cathy A. Small** (1994) Policy Lessons from Lao and Hmong Women in Thai Refugee Camps . *World Development,* 22 (7): 1045-1059.

Examines the role of Lao & Hmong women in two refugee camps in Thailand, drawing on ethnographic research. Focus is on the participation of women within the administrative structure of the camps, in camp service & training programs, & in the relocation process. While no refugees wield real power in the camps, results demonstrate how the absence of women in camp leadership & their consistent representation by men effectively muffles their potential input into camp policies, programs, or their own futures within the relocation process. This is a result, not of callous administrators nor insensitive service agencies, but rather, of the unexamined assumptions of development planning. 43 References. Adapted from the source document. (Copyright 1995, Sociological Abstracts, Inc., all rights reserved.)

46 **Chantavanich, Supang** (1996) Lao women returnees from Thailand: a neglected significant force for social and economic reintegration. In W. Giles, H. Moussa , & P. van Esterik (eds) *Development and diaspora: gender and the refugee experience.* Canada: Artemis Enterprises, pp. 208-215.

"This paper addresses the devaluation of women's productive labour among Lao women who are encouraged to take on economic pursuits in their home country, yet, as refugees, they are not allowed to continue in such roles or even have access to credit services that would enable them to invest in tools and other material."

47 **Cockburn, Cynthia** (1998) *The space between us: negotiating gender and national identities in conflict.* London/New York: Zed Books.

In this study the author focuses on understanding the processes sustaining conflict in Northern Ireland, Israel/Palestine and Bosnia/Hercegovina by means of a close involvement with three remarkable women's projects that have chosen co-operation, managing as such to create a safe space. The book re-examines theories of the self in relation to collective identities, and of gender in nationalist thought and practice. It deals with the dangers of essentialism and the problematic relationship between identity and democracy.

48 Cole, Ellen, Oliva M. Espin, & Esther Rothblum (eds) (1992) *Refugee women and their mental health: shattered societies, shattered lives.* New York: Haworth Press.

This volume is a collection of papers on the subject of mental health and overall well-being of women refugees in different regions of the world.

49 Dacyl, Janina W. (1996) Sovereignty versus Human Rights: From Past Discourses to Contemporary Dilemmas. *Journal of Refugee Studies,* 9 (2): 136-165.

"The breakdown of Communism at the end of the 1980s put into motion turbulent changes in the global system. Probably the most significant of these changes concerns the role of the sovereignty principle and human rights in international politics. It seems that these two concepts once again have been placed on a collision course with each other. This paper aims to link the evolution of the major issues of past discourse to the core post-Cold War dilemmas. Consequently, it touches upon: historical roots of the modern concept of sovereignty; the shift in the focus of sovereignty discourse and the emergence of the non-intervention principle; 'degrees' of sovereignty: absolute versus relative sovereignty; the politics of the non-intervention principle; the legality of external interference in internal matters; the status of human rights in international relations; humanitarian intervention and international relations theory. The paper ends with a tentative assessment of the challenges posed to the post-Westphalian concept of sovereignty by massive protection and assistance claims of both internally and externally displaced persons in early post-Cold War era."

50 Daley, Patricia (1991) Gender, displacement and social reproduction: settling Burundi refugees in Western Tanzania. *Journal of Refugee Studies,* 4 (3): 248-266.

"Until recently, the paucity of empirical data on refugee women has led to widespread generalization about the plight, number and condition of women in refugee communities. Discussion of refugee women tends to focus on their vulnerability and their experience as victims in acts of sexual violence and other forms of abuse. Very few studies document the less dramatic transformation of women's lives which occurs as a direct outcome of force displacement. Using evidence from primary data collected among Burundi refugees in Tanzania during 1987, the paper contends that contrary to popular perception the sex ratio African refugee settlements is much more balanced than has been assumed. This has implications for policies which associate deprivation with the predominance of women in African refugee settlements. As men and women come to terms with a redefinition of their access to resources patriarchal tendencies within the pre-migration societies and the male bias of the settlement programme combine to marginalize women from the administrative structures and, more severely, from participating in the wider Tanzanian society. Nevertheless within the restricted space of the settlement, in the absence of alternatives, both men and women have been fully integrated into the market economy as marginalized direct producers. Therefore, they are also subjected to the crises of social reproduction now facing the Tanzanian peasantry. Gender is shown to be an important, but not all encompassing, factor in the reconstruction and control over space as refugees adjust to the new environments."

51 **Daniel, Valentine E., & John Knudsen** (eds) (1995) *Mistrusting refugees.* Berkeley: University of California Press.
   The papers in this interdisciplinary volume deal with theories of trust and mistrust, and the coexistention of the two, in the context of the growing refugee problem. Some of the issues that the individual papers deal with, are: with refugees mistrusting and mistrusted, with the collapse of culturally constituted trust through the abuse of power, with the national identities of refugees and host, with the fact that trust is gendered, with the experience of trust for those tortured, with self-representation by refugees, and with the consequences for trust and protection of international refugee law.

52 **Davis, J.** (1992) The anthropology of suffering. *Journal of Refugee Studies,* 5 (2): 149-161.
   In this paper the author argues for bringing together what he calls the comfortable anthropology of social organisation and the painful anthropology of disruption and despair. He argues that 'pain is normal', in experience, in cause and in the way people deal with it. Examples: famine in Sudan, war in Italy. Suffering is part of social conditions and structures. In dealing with pain people assimilate their experience to the normal routines of pain in order to restore/preserve social order. This is what is referred to when talking

of 'cultural bereavement' with regard to refugees. Suggested consequences for anthropology: re-draw boundary between system and event; revise representations of social structure; reassess relativism and mental constructionism.

53 **Deng, Francis M.** (1995) Dealing with the Displaced: A Challenge to the International Community. *Global Governance,* 1 (1): 45-57.

The sizable international crisis triggered by internal displacement problems requires a combination of policies in order to provide international protection while reestablishing conditions for national protection. Four tasks are identified in dealing with the human rights aspect of the problem: (1) to develop country profiles in order to deal more effectively under specific circumstances; (2) to assess international law with regard to provisions for protection & assistance of the internally displaced; (3) to assess international institutions' coverage of the needs of internally displaced; & (4) to develop a global strategy based on the previous assessments. R. Jaramillo (Copyright 1995, Sociological Abstracts, Inc., all rights reserved.)

54 **DeVoe, Pamela** (1993) The silent majority: women as refugees. In R.S. Gallin, A. Ferguson, & J. Harper (eds) *The women and international development annual, vol. 3.* Boulder: Westview Press, pp. 19-52.

In her paper the author deals with the different stages of forced migration as experienced by refugee women: flight, refugee camps, resettlement. She discusses a range of gender issues that are part of these experiences, covering the topics of sexual abuse, female headed households, dependency, economic adjustment, elderly women, childbearing, mental health, gender roles in family life, and crosscuts of gender and ethnic identity. In the concluding paragraph the current research gaps with regard to women refugees are identified.

55 **Donnelly, Nancy** (1994) *Changing lives of refugee Hmong women.* Seattle: University of Washington Press.

This book deals with the lives of Hmong women refugees in resettlement in the United States. It starts with an overview of existing anthropological literature on the Hmong, and continues with an elaborate discussion of field research methods. The focus of this study is on the functioning of the family in exile as an institution, and includes an analysis of changing male and female roles. Three related chapters are on courtship, marriage and domestic violence.

56 **Dupont, Alan** (1997) Unregulated Population Flows in East Asia: A New Security. *Pacifica Review,* 9 (1): 1-22.

This paper examines the underlying causes of illegal migration and refugee movements in East Asia, and analyses their impact on the security environment of its developing states. Figures show that the number of refugees, displaced persons, and illegal labor migrants has increased dramatically in the past 20 years: 28 million people worldwide and 5 to 6 million regionally form a multiethnic migrant diaspora largely outside government control. It is argued that this large-scale, unregulated movement of people within and across national borders will increasingly occupy 21st-century foreign policy and national security establishments.

57 **Dupree, Nancy** (1990) A socio-cultural dimension: Afghan women refugees in Pakistan. In Anderson & Dupree (eds) *Cultural basis of Afghan nationalism.* London: Pinter, pp. 121-133.

This paper examines some major patterns governing the status of women in pre-exodus Afghanistan, and by doing so it highlights recent impingements on the lives of these women. The latter include impingements in Afghanistan after the installation of the leftist DRA in 1978, during the exodus, and also throughout the decade that the women have been living in exile. The paper closes with considerations of the prospects for repatriation.

58 **Dzimbiri, Lewis B.** (1995) Challenging Gender Stereotypes in Training: Mozambican Refugees in Malawi. *Development in Practice,* 5 (2): 154-157.

Contending that gender stereotyping in the recruitment of trainees for income-generating projects in refugee camps marginalizes women, it is argued that traditional gender-based approaches in the allocation of benefits be rejected in favor of a deliberate process to increase women's involvement in meaningful economic activities. These conclusions are based largely on 2 ethnographic studies of Mozambican refugees in Malawi. The first examined 2 NGOs (Non Governmental Organizations) at Chifunga Camp & 3 NGOs at Tengani Camp (based on data supplied by project coordinators & field supervisors) & found that of 1,562 beneficiaries, only 307 were women. Conversely, the Norwegian Refugee Council projects at Biriwiri & Kambironjo instituted a proactive approach to involve women in traditionally male-dominated skill areas. The results indicate that of 281 beneficiaries, 188 were women. 7 References. M. Greenberg (Copyright 1996, Sociological Abstracts, Inc., all rights reserved.)

59 **Earle, Duncan** (1994) Constructions of refugee ethnic identity: Guatemalan Mayas in Mexico and South Florida. In L.A. Camino & R.M. Krulfeld (eds) *Reconstructing lives, recapturing meaning: refugee identity, gender, and culture change.* Washington D.C.: Gordon and Breach Publishers, pp. 207-234.

This paper discusses the processes of maintaining and reconstructing ethnic identity among three populations of Mayas from Guatemala who sought refuge in Mexico and the United States. Despite substantial pressures from the surrounding dominant societies to capitulate to assimilation, each Maya group generated creative responses to its new situation without compromising the integrity of their identity. The author concludes that, for the refugees involved, self-definition and the power of autonomy are important elements in nurturing mental health as well as successful adjustment. Furthermore it is argued that the construction of identity is key to understanding social dynamics of refugee communities, and that such understanding is conditional to offering effective social assistance.

60 **Eastmond, Marita** (1996) Luchar y Sufrir-Stories of Life and Exile: Reflexions on the Ethnographic Process. *Ethnos,* 61 (3-4): 231-250.

"This paper presents in condensed form the life stories of two refugees, a man and a woman from El Salvador. The aim of collecting these and other stories has been to explore how refugees themselves make sense of the turbulent changes that war and exile force upon them. It is a way to understand political conflict and displacement through the people who live them, but also to explore the diversity of experience behind the generalised notion of 'the refugee experience'. Further, of wider ethnographic relevancies how the personal narratives mediate personal experience and cultural explanations. The present example demonstrates how a key cultural theme, grounded in a model of social experience from the home country, is employed differently by the actors to organize their narratives and understand their changing lives."

61 **Eisenbruch, Maurice** (1991) From post-traumatic stress disorder to cultural bereavement: diagnosis of Southeast Asian refugees. *Social Science and Medicine,* 33 (6): 673-680.

"There are pitfalls in the singular application of western categories in diagnosing psychiatric disorders and distress among refugees. Based on my research with Cambodian refugees I argue that cultural bereavement, by mapping the subjective experience of refugees, gives meaning to the refugee's distress, clarifies the 'structure' of the person's reactions to loss, frames psychiatric disorder in some refugees, and complements the psychiatric diagnostic categories. Cultural bereavement includes the refugees' picture – what the trauma meant to them; their cultural interpretation of symptoms commonly found among refugees that resemble post-traumatic stress disorder. Cultural bereavement may identify those people who have post-traumatic disorder on the Diagnostic and Statistical Manual (DSM) criteria but whose 'condition' is a sign of normal, even constructive, rehabilitation from devastatingly traumatic experiences. Cultural bereavement should be given appropriate status in the nosology."

62 **Engberg-Pedersen, Lars** (1997) Institutional contradictions in rural development. In C. Kay (ed) *Globalisation, competitiveness and human security.* London: Frank Cass, pp. 183-208.
"Rural development is the scene of different groups interacting on the basis of conflicting interests and strategies. Contemporary analytical approaches emphasise that actors develop strategies on the basis of their own preferences, experiences and understandings, and with reference to the constraining institutions and structures. However, they tend to ignore the symbolic aspects of institutions which provide some order in an otherwise chaotic world. Based on a study of the introduction of representative councils in four villages in Burkina Faso, this contribution argues that these symbolic aspects are important elements for understanding the changing processes of collective decision-making. Thus, new ways of organising decision-making might involve contradictions with respect to the existing institutional order."

63 **Escalona, Ana, & Richard Black** (1995) Refugees in Western Europe: Bibliographic Review and State of the Art. *Journal of Refugee Studies,* 8 (4): 364-389.
"This paper provides a concise review of the literature on recent refugee flows to western Europe. The review is organised in four sections, dealing in turn with significant areas of literature on refugees in western Europe. First, general studies are reviewed to provide background to the current situation of refugees in the region; this includes an examination of theoretical perspectives adopted by various authors, as well as considering the variety of definitions of 'refugees' that are applied at a policy-making and a theoretical level, and work on the causes of refugees flows. The second sections considers the question of the numerical significance of refugees in western Europe, as well as the geographical pattern of movement. In general, statistics are not presented in this section (although statistical sources are identified,

100 REFUGEES, GENDER AND HUMAN SECURITY

and problems with these sources commented upon); rather an overview is provided of the main trends in arrivals of refugees. Thirdly, the focus turned to recent changes in asylum policy in western European countries, including analysis of specific national trends which have continued despite moves towards harmonization of policies at a European level. Finally, the literature on settlement and integration of refugees is considered, outlining the links between national refugee settlement policies and asylum policies, as well as noting the principal themes and findings of academic research."

64 **Espin, Oliva M.** (1995) 'Race', Racism, and Sexuality in the Life Narratives of Immigrant Women. *Feminism and Psychology,* 5 (2): 223-238.
Life narratives collected from immigrant women through five individual interviews & three focus groups are used to explore how questions of national identity & sexual identity are determined & negotiated for immigrant & refugee women & the role of geography & language in understanding women's boundary & border crossings. Four life stories are discussed in detail, as illustrative of disparate adaptations to migration, & suggestions are made for future research. 51 References. Adapted from the source document. (Copyright 1995, Sociological Abstracts, Inc., all rights reserved.)

65 **Esterik, Penny van** (1996) Food and the refugee experience: gender and food in exile, asylum and repatriation. In W. Giles, H. Moussa, & P.v. Esterik (eds) *Development and diaspora: gender and the refugee experience.* Canada: Artemis Enterprises, pp. 60-73.
"In this paper the author questions the dualistic logic that pervades discussions of the food system. She examines how the right to food intersects with refugee rights and women's rights in the international discourse of human rights, and suggests that in addition to the right to be fed, we should consider the right to feed. While women's food experiences are basic to refugee survival, they seldom influence the macro-security systems that are dominated by male policy makers. By conceptualizing refugee movements as a problem of homelessness on an international scale, theoretical questions about food from a gendered perspective can be raised."

66 **Evenhuis, Winde** (1997) *De zijkant van het asielbeleid.* Utrecht: Greber/ HOM.
"In deze publicatie wordt gepleit voor een zodanige interpretatie van het Vluchtelingen verdrag dat seksespecifieke vervolging kan leiden tot toekenning van de vluchtelingenstatus. Het is een kritische analyse van het asiel-

beleid aan de hand van mensenrechtenverdragen zoals het VN-vrouwen-verdrag, en bevat aanbevelingen voor een vrouwvriendelijk asielbeleid."

67 **Falk Moore, Sally** (1994) Law in unstable settings: the dilemma of migration. In K. and F. von Benda-Beckmann & H. Marks (eds) *Coping with insecurity: an 'underall' perspective on social security in the Third World.* Special Issue Focaal 22/23, pp. 141-152.

This paper examines the alleged effectiveness and appropriateness of (inter)national law geared toward the sovereignty and monoculturalism of nation states, in the reality of a world of change in which many states and their citizens are faced with instability and insecurity. Migration is put forward as the very phenomena that illustrates the substantial unimplement-ability of many laws. The first part of the paper addresses some general arguments made about the political need for a homogeneous official culture in order to create an effective state. Secondly, the context of Burkina Faso is used as an example, being a weak state with a multiplicity of cultural forms, internal migration, economic crisis, property conflict and ethnic conflict. The author concludes that, when taking seriously the crises ahead concerning migration, property and human rights, it is time to study the limitations and uncertainties of (inter)national law and legal institutions, and examine their effectiveness in relation to particular social contexts.

68 **Fann, Patricia** (1991) The Pontic myth of homeland. *Journal of Refugee Studies*, 4 (4): 340-356.

"Since their arrival in Greece as refugees in 1922-3, the Pontic Greeks have changed their community's cultural orientation. They are no longer solely nationalistic Greeks fighting to rejoin their fortunes with the homeland, but have also become ethnicists struggling to maintain an identity within it. The shift in orientation can be traced through the changes in meaning of the Pontic slogan, *'I Romania ki an perasen, anthei kai ferei ki allo'* 'Even though our land has passed away, it will flower and bear again.' The change in orientation is also evident in the religious significance which they began to accord their quest for ethnic identity, and in the myth around which they structure their theatrical productions."

102 REFUGEES, GENDER AND HUMAN SECURITY

69 **Ferris, Elizabeth G.** (1992) Refugee women and family life. In M. McCallin (ed) *The psychological well-being of refugee children: research, practice and policy issues.* Geneva: International Catholic Child Bureau, pp. 90-105.

This paper aims to contribute to a better understanding of the psychological well-being of refugee children by looking at the situation of refugee women and family life. Four themes are addressed: the roles women play in the family and the community, and the impact of these roles on refugee children; particular problems of refugee women in exile; ways in which women's concerns can be addressed by the community and by service providers; the international policy context.

70 **Flores-Borquez, Mia** (1995) A Journey to Regain My Identity. *Journal of Refugee Studies,* 8 (1): 95-108.

"This is an analytical account of my experience as a political refugee. It covers a period of socialization in a different culture and explores the process of psychosocial transition into a state of refugeehood. I argue that in order to survive as a refugee, one has to acquire an identity that is alien to the self that made one become a political refugee. This is something that I did not do which meant that, although retaining my integrity, I had to pay a high price in other more personal terms."

71 **Frederico, J.** (1991) A well-founded fear of being persecuted? *Journal of Refugee Studies,* 4 (1): 82-92.

In this paper the author writes about his personal history and experiences as a refugee from East Timor. In his conclusion he expresses the hope that his account will in some ways be a rationale for the realisation that human tragedy cannot be measured with theoretical concepts and standard definitions. In stead these often become instruments that help to further perpetuate the hypocrisy of governments in their policies towards refugees and other marginalised groups.

72 **Getu, Haragua, & Joyce Nsubuga** (1996) Health issues affecting Sub-Saharan African women refugees. In W. Giles, H. Moussa, & P. van Esterik (eds) *Development and diaspora: gender and the refugee experience.* Canada: Artemis Enterprises, pp. 199-207.

"From the perspective of medical practitioners, the authors in this paper argue that a healthy population is a human right. They describe African refugee women as being responsible for heavy labour in refugee camps, including child rearing, food production and processing, and the provision of water and fuel usually gathered under adverse conditions. This paper makes some initial connections between the ability of women to do reproductive work and the reproduction of their own good health."

73 **Ghorashi, Halleh** (1997) Shifting and Conflicting Identities: Iranian Women Political Activists in Exile. *European Journal of Women's Studies,* 4 (3): 283-303.

Draws on interview data from 18 Iranian female political activists, ages 30-47, in exile in the Netherlands to examine how they deal with their different identities. As refugees from the Iranian Revolution of 1979, they were confronted with conflicting political, gender, & religious identities. Their escape to a new country has added a new form of conflict, ie, their position as the Iranian Other in a host country. Focus is on the changes that have occurred in various periods of their lives. How did these activists experience their lives in Iran during such drastic events as revolution, imprisonment, & living "underground?" How do they view their present lives as Iranians in exile? The impact of the past on their present lives & their views of the future is also considered. 25 References. Adapted from the source document. (Copyright 1998, Sociological Abstracts, Inc., all rights reserved.)

＊ 74 **Giles, Wenona, Helene Moussa, & Penny van Esterik (eds)** (1996) *Development and diaspora: gender and the refugee experience.* Ontario: Artemis Enterprises.

As put forward in the introduction, the papers in this volume call for a paradigm shift in refugee studies. Three challenges are envisaged: challenging feminist theory to address refugee issues; challenging advocacy literature to provide more conceptual guidelines; and challenging the study of ethnicity and migration to examine gender. The volume presents case studies of women refugees from all over the world, placed under the following main headings: theoretical considerations of feminist theory and refugee policy; reinterpreting the refugee definition; reconstructing place and identity; women refugees claiming power. Includes chapters by Indra, Giles, van Esterik, Gilad, Korac, Liebich & Ramirez, Macklin, Butler, Razack, Callamard, Getu & Nsubuga, Chantavanich, McSpadden & Moussa, McLellan, Hernandez & Garcia, Sullivan, Blakeney & Dirie & MacRae. Several of these are included separately in this annotated bibliography.

75 **Gluck, Sherna B.** (1995) Palestinian Women: Gender Politics and Nationalism. *Journal of Palestine Studies,* 24 (3[95]): 5-15.

Changes in gender discourse, consciousness, & activism since the beginning of the Palestine intifada are examined through participant observation & interviews with women's movement leaders & activists in West Bank villages & refugee camps. At the beginning of the intifada, women's independence & gender empowerment were promoted by female committee leaders, & by 1990 several women's centers & women's studies committees were established. The women's movement in Palestine aligned itself with international movements of women, but affiliation to local Palestine political factions hindered political empowerment. When the prefigurative state in occupied Palestine emerged, the predominantly male leadership neglected women's issues. The women's movement reacted with increased mobilization, but the process of state formation had factionalized the movement into those opposed & those loyal to the Palestine leadership. This split has resulted in erosion of previous gains made for women's rights. D. Generoli (Copyright 1995, Sociological Abstracts, Inc., all rights reserved.)

76 **Godfrey, Nancy, & Husein M. Mursal** (1990) International aid and national health policies: lessons from Somalia. *Journal of Refugee Studies,* 3 (2).

"Most refugees seek asylum in poor countries where health services are already inadequate. Yet, relief has focused almost exclusively on the health problems of refugees thereby neglecting the consequences of an influx of refugees and the resulting international relief operation for national health policies and services. This paper is based on analysis of national health policies for refugees in Somalia and the role of international aid in the policy process. Assumptions of temporary asylum greatly influenced policies for the organization and management of separate refugee health services. Key management strategies used to establish as separate system of basic health services which were managed and implemented by Somali nationals and refugees included centralised decision-making, standards for the organization and delivery of services and ongoing programmes for the training and supervision for health workers. International support, in the form of foreign health advisers, was essential for management by Somali officials. Nevertheless, this system was unable to ensure good health and nutritional status or the involvement of the refugees in policy and management processes. Nor was this system able to become independent of foreign aid. Thus, conclusions highlight the idealism of recommendations which focus solely on health activities or management mechanisms. Instead, there is a need for a framework which helps us to understand, explain and work within the political realities of refugee health relief operations."

77 **Gorman, Robert F.** (1994) Refugee aid and development in Africa: research and policy needs from the local perspective. In H. Adelman & J. Sorenson (eds) *African refugees: development aid and repatriation*. Boulder: Westview Press.

"This chapter examines and evaluates a decade of effort by the international community to link refugee aid and development in Africa. Drawing upon the discussions, conclusions and recommendations of the International Seminar on Refugees in Africa, held in Arusha, Tanzania, from July 30 to August 3, 1990, the chapter outlines policy recommendations and research issues needed to improve international and local efforts to link refugee and development assistance more effectively. An attempt is made here to emphasize the local African context in which this linkage must take place without ignoring the more widely studied and better understood (albeit inadequate and problematical) international mechanisms for linking refugee aid and development. Before proceeding with an evaluation of policy and proffering recommendations, it is useful to recount briefly how the refugee aid and development dialogue of the 1980s unfolded and to review the principles that emerged from it."

78 **Graham, Mark, & Shahram Khosravi** (1997) Home is where you make it: repatriation and diaspora culture among Iranians in Sweden. *Journal of Refugee Studies,* 10 (2): 115-133.

"This article examines attitudes towards returning to Iran among Iranian refugees in Sweden. Differences between Iranians are traced to various factors including economic position and political involvement. The idea of a home and a homeland, as well as that of a home culture, are critically examined in the light of the creation of a diaspora culture in Sweden and elsewhere that seeks to reconstruct aspects of Iranian culture. It is argued that not only the 'when' of return migration must be examined, but also the 'where', in a situation of dynamic cultural change which redefines the meaning of the home culture and the location of home itself."

79 **Greatbatch, Jaqueline** (1989) The gender difference: feminist critiques of refugee discourse. *International Journal of Refugee Law*, 1: 518-527.

This article critically analyzes the call by feminists for a redefinition of the persecution that acknowledges the feminist theory of social bifurcation which divides society into public and private spheres. Based on this theory, the criteria for being a refugee are drawn primarily from the male-dominated public spheres, while women's oppression which occurs in the private or domestic sphere is ignored. Thus, a redefinition of 'persecution' would give credibility to women's private sphere experiences. The adoption of a human rights-based approach is proposed, which, in recognizing women as a particular social group would include women's economic and social repression. The argument is illustrated by case studies of women in post-revolutionary Iran and under the Pinochet regime in Chile. (adapted from Neuwirth & Vincent [1997])

80 **Green, Hollyn** (1994) Refugees in transition: educational opportunity to promote the advancement of women. *Convergence,* 27 (2/3): 175-183.

In this paper the author, herself a service provider to refugees, proposes that the transitions that refugees go through as part of their flight and exile, offer a 'window of opportunity' for refugee women who should be offered educational options for the advancement of their human rights. The author sees an opportunity for positive transition in the fact that the refugee situation provides an unique time to re-examine norms and social structures that created inequality between men and women at home.

81 **Griffiths, David** (1997) Somali Refugees in Tower Hamlets: Clanship and New Identities. *New Community,* 23 (1): 5-24.

Draws on interview data from 25 Somali refugees living in Tower Hamlets in London, England, to examine C. El-Solh's 1991 & 1993 research that stressed the role of clanship as the basis of their social relations. It is argued that clanship, traditionally a system of kinship obligations, is closely related to a series of localized responses, eg, changes in the role of elders in the community & shifts in gender relations. The coexistence of tradition & innovation in relation to the interpretation of clanship is examined. 85 References. Adapted from the source document. (Copyright 1998, Sociological Abstracts, Inc., all rights reserved.)

82 **Habib, Naila** (1996) The search for home. *Journal of Refugee Studies*, 9 (1): 96-102.

This paper is a personal story in which the author tells of her experiences during the protracted civil war in Lebanon (1975-1990), during her exile in various European countries and the United States, and of her return to her home country. The author reflects on the meaning of home and the process of adaptation in exile, questioning classical assumptions related to the concepts of home and exile. She suggests it would be interesting for researchers to study how the meaning of home can facilitate or impair the adaptation of exiles and refugees over a long period of time.

83 **Haines, David W.** (1988) The pursuit of English and self-sufficiency: dilemmas in assessing refugee programme effects. *Journal of Refugee Studies*, 1 (3/4).

"In view of the inevitable after-effects of exodus and transit, most countries accepting refugees for permanent resettlement provide extensive post-arrival assistance through what are often very complex and detailed social programmes. These programmes themselves become an important factor in the adjustment of refugees to their new countries. Yet a consideration of the US experience with Southeast Asian refugees suggests that there are forbidding difficulties in documenting the specific effects that such programmes have, as separate from the effects of refugees' own efforts and of the widely varying social and economic environments in which they are resettled. These difficulties become particularly severe in the case of such a general and ambiguous programme goal as self-sufficiency."

84 **Hammond, John L.** (1993) War-Uprooting and the Political Mobilization of Central American Refugees. *Journal of Refugee Studies*, 6 (2): 105-122.

"This article examines mobilization for overt political activity, self-improvement, and productive work among four groups of war-uprooted in Central America: refugees from El Salvador and Nicaragua living in Honduras and displaced Salvadorans and Nicaraguans in their respective home countries. Modernization theory and much of the literature on refugees both suggest that their mobilization should be very low, but the level is high among Salvadoran refugees and relatively high among the internally displaced in both countries. Resource mobilization theory explains the differences among the groups in overt political mobilization, but does not explain mobilization for self-improvement and the acquisition of the skills of modernity. The differences in mobilization among the four sites can be explained by the past political experiences of each group, the perception of immediate threat, and the need for self-reliance after fleeing."

85 **Harrell-Bond, Barbara E.** (1986) *Imposing aid: emergency assistance to refugees.* Oxford/New York/Nairobi: Oxford University Press.
   This book is the first independent and thorough appraisal of an assistance programme mounted by international agencies in response to an emergency influx of refugees, in this case the Ugandans who fled to Sudan from early 1982 onward. The study is based on anthropological and participatory research methods, with data including interviews with 6,000 households – both in camps and among the great numbers of self-settled refugees who remained outside the aid 'umbrella'. The particular assistance programme considered, can be described as one of the more successful in its kind, though nevertheless the author is seriously critical about it. She does not question the need for more aid, but fundamentally questions the level of effectiveness of present approaches to assisting refugees.

86 **Harrell-Bond, Barbara E., & Ken B. Wilson** (1990) Dealing with dying: some anthropological reflections on the need for assistance by refugee relief programmes for bereavement and burial. *Journal of Refugee Studies,* 3 (3).
   "This paper explores how an anthropological understanding of death could inform relief provision so as to substantially improve the welfare of refugees. Most of the material is drawn from African examples. Even if effective assistance is provided, many refugees die during flight and exile. Using case material it is shown that despite the lack of resources, refugees continue to invest heavily in funeral and burial rites. Through lack of understanding, this behaviour often leads to conflict with relief officials. The paper argues that minimal support could make a substantial psycho-social contribution and have administrative and health benefits."

87 **Harrell-Bond, Barbara E., & Eftihia Voutira** (1992) Anthropology and the study of refugees. *Anthropology Today,* 8 (4): 6-10.
   Surveys methodological problems surrounding research on refugees & forced migrants by proposing three ways to effect the rapprochement of theoretical research & active interference in relation to issues of understanding refugee-producing crises & methods for their prevention & control. Given that most refugee situations involve cultures in violent collision, it is argued that social anthropology is best suited to assist in promoting a cross-cultural understanding of the causes & consequences of the physical act of displace-

ment & the ensuing processes of culture contact among displaced groups & host populations. Drawing from some of the recent literature on the topic of forced displacement, it is argued that anthropological research not only allows for an increased awareness of the complexity of issues involved in refugee situations (an important prerequisite for adequate policy-making decisions), but may also be used to explore & refine anthropology's own disciplinary concerns. 41 References. Modified AA (Copyright 1994, Sociological Abstracts, Inc., all rights reserved.)

88 **Harrell-Bond, Barbara E., Eftihia Voutira, & Mark Leopold** (1992) Counting the refugees: gifts, givers, patrons and clients. *Journal of Refugee Studies,* 5 (3/4).

"This paper examines the justifications, operational methods and results of the requirement to enumerate refugee populations prior to supplying food aid. The authors argue (1) that this practice is insufficient for assessing need, (2) that it leads to oppressive practices in refugee assistance, forming part of 'an ideology of control' within aid programmes, and (3) that it fails to provide the 'accountability' sought by donors. In addition, the paper questions the usual notion of 'fairness' of the distribution of welfare goods in such contexts, in the light of the anthropology of gifts, the nature of patronage systems and philosophical theories of obligation and accountability. Positive suggestions are made for ways to increase both accountability and 'client' participation in refugee food distribution systems."

89 **Hastedt, Glenn P., & Kay M. Knickrehm** (1988) Domestic violence, refugee flows, and international tension: the case of El Salvador. *Journal of Refugee Studies,* 1 (3/4).

"When viewed as a political problem rather than as a humanitarian or legal issue, refugee flows present many potential challenges to state policy-makers. Challenges to decision-making autonomy are among the most significant of these. Such challenges arise because of the ability of refugee flows to exacerbate international tensions and contribute to increased levels of domestic violence. They pose an especially severe problem where political development is weak and the expansion of state autonomy is a critical issue for policy-makers. In states that are hostile to one another, it is obvious that refugee flows are likely to take on a political rather than humanitarian dimension. The receiving state will at the very least use the refugees for propaganda purposes. It might be expected that when the sending and receiving states are friendly or at least ideologically compatible, any response to refugees will be humanitarian in nature. However, where the cause of the refugee flow is domestic repression and violence, the response to the flow is likely to be politicized. The tensions accompanying refugee flows can be organized around the issue of decision-making autonomy. By far those tensions surrounding foreign policy options present the greatest potential for creating and exacerbating regional tension, because they most directly involve the refugee in the power calculations made by states regarding their ability to realize national security whenever possible. By emphasizing threats to security, they can unite elite groups and justify repressive solutions to problems. Refugees fleeing repression in a neighbouring state present challenges to decision-making autonomy and potentially threaten national security in the receiving state. To the extent that policy-makers in the receiving state have developed a habit of geopolitical thinking, they are likely to respond to the refugees primarily as a threat to national security. The most immediate victims are the refugees themselves, but the potential is created for increased regional violence. This phenomenon is illustrated by the flow of refugees from El Salvador into Honduras."

90 **Hathaway, James C.** (1991) Reconceiving refugee law as human rights protection. *Journal of Refugee Studies,* 4 (2).

"This paper proceeds from the view that refugee law is fundamentally a means of reconciling the national self-interest of powerful states to the inevitability of involuntary migration. As industrialized states have become increasingly dissatisfied with the attentiveness of the Convention-based refugee law system to their exclusionary objectives, the reform of refugee law has been placed on the international agenda in a variety of fora. The paper suggests that it may be possible to re-orient the reform movement towards an alignment of refugee law with international human rights law. This requires that the current regime be re-focused on the restoration of the refugee's rights to community membership, and that a binding system of inter-state obligation be enacted to ensure temporary asylum. By defining the duty of protection beyond the first asylum stage to be a function of the relative resources and absorptive capacities of states, it is posited that the substantive scope of refugee law could simultaneously be extended to a significantly broader class of involuntary migrant than at present."

91 **Hendrie, Barbara** (1991) The politics of repatriation: the Tigrayan refugee repatriation 1985-1987. *Journal of Refugee Studies*, 4 (2): 200-218.

"The paper examines the political and operational issues involved in the organized repatriation of some 200,000 Tigrayan refugees from eastern Sudan to areas of northern Ethiopia controlled by the Tigray Peoples Liberation Front (TPLF). Due to the sensitivity of refugee returns to territories controlled by 'non-recognized entities', the United Nations High Commission for Refugees (UNHCR) neither formally recognized nor actively supported the movement. In the absence of UNHCR's sanctioning of the repatriation, locally-based initiatives for support became problematic. The failure to provide adequate assistance to returnees, especially recovery inputs, had negative implications for food production in Tigray for this population over the next several years."

92 **Herdt, Tom de, & Stefaan Marysse** (1997) Against all odds: coping with regress in Kinshasa, Zaire. In C. Kay (ed) *Globalisation, competitiveness and human security.* London: Frank Cass, pp. 209-130.

"Drawing on a field-survey carried out in the city of Kinshasa, the authors aimed to gain more insight into the (re)-activation of solidarity networks in times of economic crisis. Solidarity networks, it is argued, have differential impact on socio-professional groups and hence one should be very cautious about making 'general' statements on their (dys)functional character. Hence, it remains unclear whether the overall informalisation of Kinshasa's economic structure can explain the fact that in the midst of overall regress in Zaire, the inhabitants of its capital city seem to have been able to consolidate their position."

93 **Hernandez, Guadalupe G., & Natividad Garcia** (1996) Mama Maquin refugee women: participation and organisation. In W. Giles, H. Moussa, & P.van Esterik (eds) *Development and diaspora: gender and the refugee experience.* Canada: Artemis Enterprises, pp. 258-267.

"This paper deals with the Mama Maquin foundation founded by Guatamalan refugee women in Mexico, of which the authors are members. The paper illustrates how women become agents of change in their own lives. In exile, the women have gained a new sense of consciousness about their potential and have learned how to organize. Two years after being founded, Mama Maquin boasts 8000 members from three states in Mexico. Not only are the members active in decisions about camp life, they also have played an important part in the repatriation agreement to Guatemala. One

REFUGEES, GENDER AND HUMAN SECURITY

112

of the reasons the exile experience of Guatamalan women was different from other nationality/country groups is that their aboriginal culture is strongly based in a collective way of life. This facilitated a re-creation of their way of life in refugee camps."

94 **Hiegel, Jean P.** (1994) Use of indigenous concepts and healers in the care of refugees: some experiences from the Thai border camps. In A. Marsella et al. (eds) *Amidst peril and pain: the mental health and well-being of the world's refugees.* Washington D.C.: American Psychological Association, pp. 293-310.

The author offers a discussion of the use of indigenous healers in refugee health care. His experiences treating Khmer refugees in Thai border camps are reflected in the detailed knowledge he offers regarding the many positive roles that indigenous healers can play in refugee care. His discussion of resistance to the use of indigenous healers from Western physicians and allied professionals serves as an example of the ethnocentricity that often characterizes well-intentioned Western health care providers.

95 **Hieronymi, Otto** (1996) The evasion of state responsibility and the lessons from Rwanda: the need for a new concept of collective security. *Journal of Refugee Studies,* 9 (3): 236-239.

There is currently widespread concern not only about existing conflicts in Rwanda and other parts of the world but also about the possible outbreak and multiplication of new conflicts resulting from bad governments, i.e. governments in which oppression and corruption have made the political system incapable of providing an adequate framework for the reconciliation of conflicts. The author argues in favour of a new approach, termed collective security.

96 **Hitchcox, Linda** (1990) *Vietnamese refugees in Southeast Asian camps.* London: Macmillan.

This book records the experiences of Vietnamese refugees who fled their homeland after the fall of Saigon in 1975 and who have been staying for months or years in the first asylum camps in Southeast Asia. The study is anthropological in nature and based on the situation in 1987. It gives a detailed analysis of the bureaucratic machinery of assistance and of the refugees' struggle to be accepted for resettlement. In the conclusion to her book, the author once more emphasises the disparity between how the refugees see themselves and the way they are defined by the authorities by means of reductionist labels. This is linked to theories about power and control by Goffman and Foucault.

97 **Hollands, Marlie** (1998) *Nieuwe ruimte. Integratie als avontuur.* Utrecht: Uitgeverij Jan van Arkel.
"Dit boek is gebaseerd op gesprekken met voormalige vluchtelingen over de wijze waarop zij in Nederland een nieuw leven hebben opgebouwd. De auteur laat zich door deze gesprekken inspireren om na te denken over deze samenleving, over de veranderingen die daarin plaatsvinden en over de betekenis van integratie vanuit haar perspectief als hier geboren Nederlandse. Zij pleit ervoor integratie te beschouwen als een avontuur. Een maatschappelijk avontuur waarbij we allemaal betrokken zijn, gevestigde Nederlanders net zo goed als vluchtelingen of andere nieuwkomers."

98 **Hondagneu-Sotelo, Pierrette** (1994) *Gendered transitions: Mexican experiences of immigration.* Berkeley: University of California Press.
In this study the author analyzes how the intersection of micro and macro forces shapes the migration and settlement of Mexican undocumented immigrant women and men in a Northern California community. The study is situated within the relevant literature and debates of various disciplines, including feminist theory. Following chapters deal with issues of how gender relations in families and social networks shape diverse migration patterns for men and women; how gender relations are renegotiated and reconstructed in exile; and how these new gender arrangements motivate immigrant women to prolong and consolidate family settlement.

99 **Indra, Doreen M.** (1988) An Analysis of the Canadian Private Sponsorship Program for Southeast Asian Refugees. *Ethnic Groups,* 7 (2): 153-172.
Consequences of the Canadian program for refugee adjustment, in which refugee families are financially supported by groups of individuals or by religious or other institutions, are reviewed. Private sponsorship via this program grew following its inception in 1978, until at the peak flow of Southeast Asian refugees (1981), about 50% of all migrants were participating. Preliminary expectations were that private sponsorship would serve social, psychological, educational, & financial purposes, but data from a Vancouver-based survey of 1,348 refugees showed that even daily contact with sponsors did not mean significant differences in employment status, English language fluency, or knowledge of Canadian society, when private-sponsored refugees were compared with government-sponsored ones. A model is

developed for the argument that structural constraints in the initial formulation of relations between refugees & sponsors (limited cross-cultural tools, sponsorship monopoly on power, the lack of role models for sponsor-refugee relations, & overall sexism) led to social conflicts between refugees & sponsors, refugee sense of deprivation, & refugee female subordination. 1 Figure, 41 References. Adapted from the source document. (Copyright 1992, Sociological Abstracts, Inc., all rights reserved.)

100 **Indra, Doreen M.** (1989) Ethnic human rights and feminist theory: gender implications for refugee studies and practice. *Journal of Refugee Studies,* 2 (2): 221-242.

"Over the past ten years, many individuals and institutions providing humanitarian assistance to refugees have asserted a commitment to increasing the participatory input of refugees, especially women. Refugee research has also begun to stress the practical need for greater refugee input. Also, while still a minor element in refugee studies, inquiry concerning refugee women is on the upswing. However, the uncritical acceptance of liberal participatory democratic ideology presently impedes the drive to increase effective refugee participation, especially on the part of women. It also places an unrealistically narrow and biased constraint on the analysis of women and gender structures in refugee studies. A feminist analysis of liberal democratic philosophy and practice is outlined, and is exemplified by a Canadian instance of representative ethnic rights advocacy. These have a number of implications for how both refugee studies and humanitarian assistance address issues of women, gender and participation, which are outlined in conclusion."

101 **Indra, Doreen M.** (1991) Some anthropological qualifications on the effects of ethnicity and social change on mental health. *Sante, Culture, Health,* VIII (1/2): 7-32.

"In this paper I address six stereotypic assumptions about how social change affects the mental health of people in Canada identified as 'ethnic'. My attention is not primarily focussed on immigrant, refugee and other 'ethnic' women, men and children *per se,* but rather on the social problem/ social issue discourse in which they are often framed. I show how premises of this order of abstraction are far too general and monolithic to contribute much to understanding the mental health dynamics of particular individuals and groups, and in particular obscure important inter-personal and inter-group differences in how people react to changing situations. In a concluding section, I extend the discussion beyond these six points to address briefly some overall limitations of placing immigrants and refugees in a discourse that foregrounds personal and social problems."

102 **Indra, Doreen M.** (1996) Some feminist contributions to refugee studies. In W. Giles, H. Moussa, & P. van Esterik (eds) *Development and diaspora: gender and the refugee experience.* Canada: Artemis Enterprises, pp. 30-43.

"In this paper the author explores some of the ways that feminist discourse and ideas have been and might be applied to refugee research. She raises issues surrounding diversity, cultural relativism and identity, and 'different feminisms'. Regarding the latter, the author considers how feminist theory is related to the location of the theorist and her own experiences. She particularly questions how the term 'refugee' – developed through bureaucratic discourse – is often adopted in an unquestioning manner by researchers, practitioners and advocates."

103 **Inowlocki, Lena, Helma Lutz, Serin Erengezgin, & Neval Gultekin** (1998) *Analysis of an Autobiographical Interview with a Migrant Woman Laborer, as a Document of a Group's Case Interpretation.* Association Paper.

In a discussion regarding biographical research, based on an interview with a migrant woman laborer named Hulya, focus is on the following points: (1) the reconstruction of sedimented life experience in Hulya's account & the relationship to what is thematized & emphasized by her; (2) the biographical work of dealing with expectations & demands on her as a cheap, temporary, speechless work slave in contrast to her self-perception, & her ensuing contrastive positioning & action against processes of social exclusion, humiliation, & exploitation; (3) an analysis of Hulya's expressiveness in shaping her account & her self-presentation, eg, by means of irony & distancing, especially with regard to the multiple lines of trajectory in work situations & illness, which have, notwithstanding their effect on her life, been shaped into tentative action schemes; (4) consequences for the discussion of theoretical concepts, eg, biographical work, through an analysis of biographical reflexivity that might be specific to biographical processes of migration; & (5) suggestions for the interpretation of biographical interviews through insights gained in the course of group discussions having to do with the combination of resources of the group members, eg, their respective contextual & situated knowledge. (Copyright 1998, Sociological Abstracts, Inc., all rights reserved.)

104 **Jaksic, Ivan** (1994) In search of safe haven: exile, immigration and identity. In R. Benmayor & A. Skotnes (eds) *International yearbook of oral history and life stories, vol. III, migration and identity*. New York: Oxford University Press, pp. 19-33.

In this paper the author, a refugee from Chile in the United Sates, communicates her personal experiences of exile, especially of the years just before and after leaving Chile in the mid 1970s. Issues of communication, language, memory and identity are central.

105 **Johnson, Peter, & Sabah El-Hato** (1993) A three-year study of community-wide trauma: adults' self-reported experiences, emotional reactions, and feeling states. *Journal of Refugee Studies*, 6 (4): 389-402.

"In each of three years, 1989-1991, Palestinians in the Gaza Strip (N=101, 159, 158) completed questionnaires concerning their experiences and emotions during the popular uprising against the military occupation. Respondents provided information on their potentially traumatic experiences, the intensity of resulting emotions, their symptoms of stress, and methods of coping. Results are examined in the context of the waxing and waning of community support for the resistance movement."

106 **Kathina, Monica** (1996) Access to resources and the right to work: a call for a gender-sensitive legal framework in situations of internal displacement. In *Legal status of refugee and internally displaced women in Africa*. Nairobi, Kenya: UNIFEM/AFWIC, pp. 253-265.

This paper deals with the experiences and situation of internally displaced women in the western province of Kenya. It is argued that access to resources and the right to work is fundamental to the enjoyment of other rights and, therefore, any gender-specific legal instruments that intend to protect and empower internally displaced women ought to address these issues. The authors presentation is based on observations of an on-going evaluation of the resettlement programme of a formerly displaced population as undertaken by the Centre for Refugee Studies, Moi University, Kenya.

• 107 **Kay, Christóbal (ed)** (1997) *Globalisation, competitiveness and human security*. London: Frank Cass Ltd.

In this collection of articles the connections between globalisation, competitiveness and human security are explored as well as their relevance for development studies. The first six papers address the theoretical issues involved in this broad research subject, focusing attention on – amongst others – the following questions: How does the process of globalisation combined with a growing international competitiveness affect people's lives? Does the rise of regionalism complement processes of trade liberalisation, thereby fostering globalisation, or does it fragment the world economy into trading blocs which hinder further globalisation? Will regionalism provide human security in the future? Can globalisation be interpreted as a project of Western cultural domination? Should decentralisation be welcomed as an effective way of enhancing people's participation in a globalising world? The following four papers deal with these theoretical issues more indirectly by means of case studies in Asia, Africa and Latin America. These latter papers by Berner, Engberg-Pedersen, de Herdt and Wilson are included separately in this annotated bibliography.

108 **Kay, Diana** (1987) *Chileans in exile: private struggles, public lives.* MacMillan Press: London.

"Based on in-depth interviews, this book gives and interpretive account of how a group of Chileans now living in Scotland have rebuilt their lives in exile after the Chilean military coup of September 1973. Incorporating a gender dimension, the study found that while both women and men in Chile were politically active, they experienced difficulties with the authorities at different times. Men tended to encounter problems during the military coup, while women suffered greatly after the junta began to persecute individuals believed to be involved in anti-state activities. After fleeing Chile for Scotland, women continued their political activities with more frequency than men, thus requiring men to stay home and assist with the household chores and child care. The reversal in gender roles experienced during resettlement is discussed in terms of its capacity to challenge traditional gender roles in Chilean society." (taken from Neuwerth & Vincent [1997])

109 **Kay, Diana** (1988) The politics of gender in exile. *Sociology,* 22 (1): 1-21.

"This article explores the experiences of Chilean men and women exiled in Britain since the military overthrow of the Popular Unity government in September 1973. The study, based on in-depth interviews, examines the very different accounts of exile given by men and women. These gender differences in accounting are related to men's and women's different location and involvement in public and private spheres. During a period of accelerated social change – from a period of socialist experimentation and a military dictatorship in Chile to exile in a developed capitalist country – both public and private spheres undergo dramatic quantitative and qualitative shifts. This study highlights the impact of these shifts for relations between men and women exiles. It is argued that public and private spheres were brought into a new and more conflictual relationship in exile, politicising areas of life which had been largely unexamined during Popular Unity. The impact of these changes for women's experiences of subordination in the home and marriage and on women's ability to formulate their grievances as public issues are explored."

110 **Kearney, M.** (1995) The Local and the Global: The Anthropology of Globalization and Transnationalism. *Annual Review of Anthropology,* 24 (547-565.): -565.

Examines current anthropological literature concerned with migration & other forms of population movement, & with the movement of information, symbols, capital, & commodities in global & transnational spaces. Special attention is given to the significance of contemporary increases in the volume & velocity of such flows for the dynamics of communities & the identity of their members. Also examined are innovations in anthropological theory & forms of representation that are responses to such nonlocal contexts & influences. 141 References. Adapted from the source document. (Copyright 1996, Sociological Abstracts, Inc., all rights reserved.)

111 **Kearney, Robert N., & Barbara D. Miller** (1988) Suicide and Internal Migration in Sri Lanka. *Journal of Asian and African Studies,* 23 (3-4): 287-304.

Official statistics are used to examine whether the rise of suicide rates in Sri Lanka in recent decades is attributable to the disruptions caused by increased levels of internal migration. Analysis of rates by sex for the nation, district, & age groups reveals that, while internal migration cannot explain completely the universal rise in suicide in Sri Lanka, there is a strong association between suicide & internal migration, particularly in the dry zone districts where migrants comprise 50% of the population in most adult age groups. 6 Tables, 3 Figures. Modified HA (Copyright 1989, Sociological Abstracts, Inc., all rights reserved.)

112 **Keely, Charles B.** (1992) The Resettlement of Women and Children Refugees. *Migration World Magazine,* 20 (4): 14-18.

Although women & children comprise about 80% of refugee populations under UN care, they account for only 57%-70% of refugees resettled in major recipient countries (the US, Canada, & Australia), & their particular needs are often not met. The bias toward adult males is probably a consequence of the UN convention definition of "refugee." A woman refugee is less likely than a man to be at risk of persecution for her own political activities & thus less likely to be classified as a refugee to be resettled. Women are more likely to be fleeing war or at persecution risk because of their husbands' activities. Quotas are not recommended to ensure the resettlement of more women, because the goal should continue to be saving the most vulnerable refugees. This requires situational judgments. 2 Tables, 2 Photographs. E. Blackwell (Copyright 1994, Sociological Abstracts, Inc., all rights reserved.)

113 **Kelly, Nancy** (1994) Guidelines for women's asylum claims. *International Journal of Refugee Law, 6* (4): 517-534.

"These *guidelines* provide a framework for analyzing and interpreting the claims of women asylum seekers as well as guidance for interviewing women applicants and assessing the evidence they present. Two broad categories of gender-related claims are identified: those where persecution constitutes a *type* of harm that is particular to the applicant's gender, such as rape or genital mutilation; and those where the persecution may be imposed *because of* the applicant's gender, for example, because of the woman's violations of societal norms. The *Guidelines* provide an analysis of the individual components in the refugee definition incorporated in the United States Immigration and Naturalization Act (which is substantially that provided by the 1951 Convention / 1967 Protocol), looks at evidentiary issues of particular relevance to women claimants, and finally offers procedural considerations for the adjudication of women's cases. They are intended to serve as a supplemental tool for assessing the claims of women who apply for asylum in the United States, but given the international dimensions to refugee protection, are also likely to be helpful in other jurisdictions."

114 **Khasiani, Shanyisa A.** (1990) The Role of Education and Training in the Local Integration of Women Refugees in Kenya. *African Urban Quarterly, 5* (3-4): 269-275.

Questionnaire data from 445 women refugees in Kenya suggest that education & training do not have as great a potential for promoting their local integration as has been assumed, primarily because extant educational & training programs cannot meet the needs of the large numbers of refugees. Some women do not even know of their existence. These programs must be expanded, & this is an international responsibility; the countries of asylum cannot cope alone. International agencies should establish aggressive outreach programs that reach & inform more women refugees. 6 Tables, 18 References. Adapted from the source document. (Copyright 1994, Sociological Abstracts, Inc., all rights reserved.)

115 **Kibreab, Gaim** (1993) The Myth of Dependency among Camp Refugees in Somalia 1979-1989. *Journal of Refugee Studies,* 6 (4): 321-349.
"This paper examines first the factors that led to the institutionalization of refugee camps in Somalia which were initially established en route to durable solutions. Second, it challenges the stereotypes that had contributed to wrong perceptions among the aid agencies particularly with regard to the alleged prevalence of the so-called 'dependency syndrome' among the camp refugees between 1979 and 1989. The findings here show not only the dearth of evidence for such a phenomenon, but also that within the given constraints and limited opportunities, the refugees were found to be imaginative, resourceful and industrious. In spite of the unfavourable conditions, the refugees succeeded in maintaining their independence and cultural identity."

116 **Kibreab, Gaim** (1995) Eritrean Women Refugees in Khartoum, Sudan, 1970-1990. *Journal of Refugee Studies,* 8 (1): 1-25.
"This paper discusses the changing roles of women in Eritrean society and assesses the impacts of the refugee experience on Eritrean women in Khartoum by looking at the adjustments they have made to life in exile. The findings show that they have experienced loss of traditional roles, responsibilities and supportive networks. The majority are former urban dwellers and they were not, therefore, socialized for an independent livelihood. However, their cultural backgrounds and the institutional constraints operative in the country of asylum notwithstanding, they exhibit remarkable openness to change and to assuming new and unfamiliar roles in an environment characterized by malevolence to women's independence and self-assertion. The factors that predispose them to adapt to downward status mobility, the roles they play in sustaining the lives of their relatives/friends and the sufferings they experience are examined."

ANNOTATED BIBLIOGRAPHY 121

117 **Kibreab, Gaim** (1996) *Ready and willing... but still waiting: Eritrean refugees in Sudan and the dilemmas of return.* Uppsala, Sweden: Life and Peace Institute.

"Starting from a critique of the assumption that voluntary repatriation is solely a function of political changes in the country of origin, this book offers a deeper and more complex picture of the dilemmas facing Eritrean refugees in the Sudan. In countries such as Eritrea where human displacement is the result of an interplay between political, economic, social, military and environmental factors there are a host of circumstances which combine to make voluntary repatriation a far from simple solution. The author argues that it is precisely these factors, particularly economic vulnerability and instability, that international agencies, host and donor governments alike need to address if programmes of voluntary repatriation are ultimately to succeed in Eritrea."

118 **Kibreab, Gaim** (1997) Environmental Causes and Impact of Refugee Movements: A Critique of the Current Debate. *Disasters,* 21 (1): 20-38.

Relationships among insecurity, environmental change, & population displacement are discussed, arguing that environmental change & concomitant population displacement are the consequences of war & insecurity rather than triggers for it. The state of knowledge concerning the impact of refugees on the environment of host countries is critically reviewed to demythologize some of its aspects that have, through repetition, become accepted as scientific truth. 71 References. Adapted from the source document. (Copyright 1998, Sociological Abstracts, Inc., all rights reserved.)

119 **Knudsen, Are, & Kate Halvorsen** (1997) Income-generating programmes in Pakistan and Malawi: a comparative review. *Journal of Refugee Studies,* 10 (4): 462-475.

"This paper reviews income-generating programmes in Pakistan and Malawi organized by the Norwegian Refugee Council (NRC). It compares the different strategies chosen by the NRC regarding project design and the creation of efficient income-generating programmes for refugees. In Pakistan the project design and implementation focused on training and support to income-generating activities based on the traditional artisan skills of mainly men. In Malawi the programme approach was less conventional as the gender issue was high on the agenda, but the aim of targeting women was constrained by poor project design and implementation. The paper discusses problems involved in creating programmes which can enhance the income of refugees, increase their skills and contribute to self-sufficiency in the country of asylum and eventually upon repatriation."

120 **Knudsen, John** (1991) Therapeutic strategies for refugee coping. *Journal of Refugee Studies,* 4 (1): 21-38.

"In order to cope with their life in transit and exile, refugees have to learn not only how to reduce the stress which results from disruption in their way of life, but also how to come to terms with relief programmes set up to help them. The refugees regard therapeutic intervention as a threat, since a diagnosis may have dramatic consequences for their future. Silence and withdrawal seem safer strategies than talk and self revelation. Paradoxically, the relief workers' therapeutic strategies, while decreasing their own stress, may serve to intensify that of the refugees."

121 **Kok, Walter** (1989) Self-settled refugees and the socio-economic impact of their presence on Kassala, Eastern Sudan. *Journal of Refugee Studies,* 2 (4).

"The article is based on findings of a research study on the impact of spontaneously settled Eritrean refugees on the town of Kassala and its surrounding area, which are constituent parts of the border region in eastern Sudan. The main conclusion is that the congeniality of the hosting area determines the survival strategies of self-settled refugees. Needless to say, in the Kassala region, region specific factors have mitigated the socio-economic and socio-cultural burden of refugees. In the light of the study's findings, the alleged helplessness of the refugee is considered a myth. It is recommended that the Sudanese Government designate distinct regions – such as Kassala region – for the settlement of refugees. The prevalent policy of the Sudanese Government, and also of UNHCR, to invest most of the funds for the accommodation of refugees in planned settlements, is questioned."

122 **Korac, Maja** (1996) Understanding Ethnic-National Identity and Its Meaning: Questions from Women's Experience. *Women's Studies International Forum,* 19 (1-2): 133-143.

"This article examines the meaning of ethnic-national identity focusing on author's personal search for ethnic-national identity or location in the context of the disintegration of Yugoslavia. From that point of departure, the author analysis the position and role of women within ethnic-national discourses in what was Yugoslavia. This article challenges the essentialist notion of belonging to ethnic-national collective and its links to the patriarchal values of brotherhood and solidarity, examining the way that the discourse of male violence and ethnic-nationalism works in relation to gender. It argues for deconstruction and rearticulation of such male-defined maps of belonging, suggesting a more inclusive politics of ethnic-national identity which would allow for allegiances based on acts of conscious political choice and acknowledgement of internal differences."

123 **Krulfeld, Ruth M.** (1992) Cognitive mapping and ethnic identity: the changing concept of community and nationalism in the Laotian diaspora. In P.A. DeVoe (ed) *Selected papers on refugee issues.* Washington D.C.: American Anthropological Association, pp. 4-26.

"Refugees, the victims of forced and usually unplanned change, must rapidly establish their recreated, newly created and negotiated communities, cultures and identities in their new homelands. It is contended here that people make cognitive maps of their communities and identities, in which symbols are used to demarcate ethnic boundaries and to denote changes in their identities. Symbols can therefore be used to trace such changes as refugees respond to on-going circumstances, both in host countries and countries of origin. A longitudinal study and a survey that considers sociocultural variability within a lowland Lao refugee population are used here to trace the process of transformations in ethnic and national identities."

124 **Krulfeld, Ruth M.** (1994) Buddhism, maintenance and change: reinterpreting gender in a Lao refugee community. In L.A. Camino & R.M. Krulfeld (eds) *Reconstructing lives, recapturing meaning: refugee identity, gender and culture change.* Washington D.C.: Gordon and Breach Publishers, pp. 97-128.

This paper deals with the issue of changing gender roles and identities in refugee communities through a study of Laotian refugees in the United States, in particular a Buddhist Monk and Nun. The study shows how understanding (the value assigned to) gender roles is crucial to understanding change and adjustment in refugee communities. Interestingly, it shows that certain changes in gender roles and concepts – changes initiated by the Nun – permit the maintenance of an area of culture important to Lao refugee ethnic identity: Buddhist religion and tradition. The author suggests that Lao women may be less conservative in negotiating new religious gender roles. At the same time she stresses that the roles of the Monk and the Nun are reciprocal and complimentary and concludes that in this case culture change

124 REFUGEES, GENDER AND HUMAN SECURITY

and culture maintenance may be seen as part of the same dynamic process of renegotiating and continuing a Lao ethnic identity.

125 **Krznaric, Roman** (1997) Guatemalan Returnees and the Dilemma of Political Mobilization. *Journal of Refugee Studies,* 10 (1): 61-78.
"This paper examines political conflict within communities of Guatemalan returnees. It challenges assumptions regarding the cohesion and homogeneity of such communities. An analysis of conflict in one particular community is broadened to illustrate generalized internal conflict amongst returnees on a regional level and in local politics. The source of conflict is traced to the effects of political organization and awareness-raising (particularly amongst women) which occurred while the refugees were in refugee camps in Mexico, conflict over resources and differing attitudes to cooperation with the national government, the private sector and popular forces on the Guatemalan left. The final section of the paper examines the consequences of the internal conflict with regard to the returnees' struggle for land, the possibility of overcoming the culture of fear and insecurity linked to the civil war, opportunities for obtaining development funds, and the place of women in the decision-making structures and processes of the communities."

126 **Kuhlman, Tom** (1991) The economic integration of refugees in developing countries: a research model. *Journal of Refugee Studies,* 4 (1): 1-20.
"Although the number of empirical studies on the integration of refugees is increasing rapidly, there is a dearth of theoretical reflection – at least as far as the specific problems of coping with refugee flows in the Third World are concerned. This article outlines a theoretical framework for research on refugee integration. Its specific aim is to design a model for economic integration, but this is seen as only one aspect of a general integration process. After a critical discussion of insights from migration and acculturation theory, a definition of integration is proposed and a comprehensive model of integration outlined. Next, economic aspects of the model are identified and a separate model specifying their interrelationships is formulated."

127 **Kuhlman, Tom** (1994) *Asylum or aid? : the economic integration of Ethiopian and Eritrean refugees in the Sudan.* London: Avebury.
Using the case of Ethiopian and Eritrean refugees in the Sudan, the author describes and analyses the factors that influence the economic integration of refugees in the country of asylum. These include characteristics of the

refugees themselves, circumstances surrounding the flight process, conditions pertaining in the host country, policies adopted by various actors to deal with the consequences of refugee influx, the history of refugee settlement in the host country, and noneconomic elements. Two different dimensions of the integration process are recognized, namely its effect on the host society and its effect on the refugees. Fieldwork was carried out in 1986-1987 in eastern Sudan, in Kassala and the surrounding rural area. The author concludes, amongst others, that aid as determined by its donors has not really helped the refugees in question, nor has it been successful in reducing the burden they impose on the host country. The refugees suffer from a lack of legal rights, and the rights which they do have are violated. In that perspective, asylum, not aid, becomes the central consideration in dealing with refugee issues.

128 **Kulig, Judith C.** (1994) Old traditions in a new world: changing gender relations among Cambodian refugees. In L.A. Camino & R.M. Krulfeld (eds) *Reconstructing lives, recapturing meaning: refugee identity, gender and culture change.* Washington D.C.: Gordon and Breach Publishers, pp. 129-146.

This paper explores changing concepts of gender roles and identities in refugee communities through a study of Cambodian refugees in the United States. The author argues that, although on the surface Cambodian gender relations appear static, they are in fact covertly though actively being renegotiated in resettlement. Women have always been essential in Cambodian social order because they are the ones responsible for 'holding their culture'. Therefore, in resettled communities in the United States there is a lot of concern regarding Cambodian women's behavior. Men feel threatened by the greater economic independence of refugee women, as well as suffer from loss of self esteem. The women are seen as changing too rapidly, and their increased exercise of autonomy in gender behavior carries with it the blame for loss of ethnic identity. The women use subtle methods in attempting to instill changes, while the men use overt means to control their wives and daughters.

129 **Kwok Bun, Chan, & Kenneth Christie** (1995) Past, present and future: the Indochinese refugee experience twenty years later. *Journal of Refugee Studies,* 8 (1): 75-94.

"This review of research on refugees from Southeast Asia begins with an examination of the conceptual and definitional problems pertaining to the question 'who is a refugee?', as worked out in the Southeast Asian context. It considers the political, sociological and psychological aspects of the total refugee experience: in transit from Indochina, in camps, in countries of re-settlement, and in repatriation, voluntary and forced. With regard to a future research agenda on the Indochinese experience(s), the essay focuses on the unfolding identity options on offer to the Indochinese whilst they are articulating their proper place within the triangular framework of the host societies (present), the emerging Indochinese diasporas (future), and their homelands back in Southeast Asia (past)."

130 **Lal, Victor** (1997) From reporter to refugee: the politics of asylum in great Britain. *Journal of Refugee Studies,* 10 (1): 79-90.

In this paper the author – writer, academic and refugee from Fiji – recounts his seven year battle with the British government for political asylum and what he calls its destructive force on human dignity and human rights. A more extensive account of the author's experiences is published by the Refugee Studies Programme and Worldview Publications, Oxford, March 1997.

131 **Larkin, Mary A., Frederick Cuny, & Barry e. Stein** (1991) *Repatriation under conflict in Central America.* Washington D.C./Dallas: CIPRA/Intertect Institute.

This volume examines repatriation in the Central American context by means of three case studies that deal with the motivations of Nicaraguan, Guatamalan and Salvadoran refugees from their initial flight through repatriation. These highlight the motivations of refugees to repatriate by their own means, i.e. outside of formal tripartite agreements. It furthermore shows how many refugees chose to return to their homelands – even when the political, economic and social factors that made them flee have not yet disappeared – rather than to live under dire camp conditions at the mercy of outside control and with the threat of forced relocation. However, when these refugees repatriate informally, they have no recourse to protection and assistance like formal returnees. The author recommends an increased focus in international research on the problems related to so-called unofficial refugees and returnees, in the first place for these people themselves.

132 **Lavik, N. et al.** (1996) A refugee protest action in a host country: possibilities and limitations of an intervention by a mental health unit. *Journal of Refugee Studies,* 9 (1): 73-88.

"In February 1994, a group of Bosnian refugees left their reception centre, prescribed by the refugee authorities in Norway, and settled at the Central Railway Station in Oslo as a protest action against their conditions at the reception centre. The episode immediately attracted much media interest, and the Psychosocial Centre for Refugees at the University of Oslo was asked by the Directorate of Immigration to make an examination and evaluation of the refugees. After the Centre had ensured that such an evaluation was explicitly wanted by the refugees themselves, the whole group of 37 adults were individually examined by psychiatrists and psychologists. Ten children were observed separately. The findings showed that almost all the members of the group had experienced extreme traumatization and suffered from various post-traumatic symptoms. The findings were reported back to the Directorate of Immigration, and the refugees were kept informed. The possibilities and ethical dilemmas involved in this type of psychiatric intervention in a conflict between refugees and political authorities are discussed."

133 **Leach, Melissa** (1992) *Dealing with displacement: refugee-host relations, food and forest resources in Sierra Leonean Mende communities during the Liberian influx,* 1990-91. Brighton: Institute of Development Studies.

This report, which is based on research carried out in the Gola forest area of Sierra Leone (1991), examines how refugees from the civil war in Liberia were accommodated within rural communities during the subsequent year, and its implications for food security and for the environment. It shows that, while aid agencies in general are unused to 'self-settled' refugee situations, for local people historical and recent cross-border ties, kinship relations and prevailing attitudes towards 'strangers' made this an obvious approach. Local views of refugees differed from categorization by agencies: while the latter focused on nationality, host-refugee relations were structured according to differential geographical, kinship and ethnolinguistic boundaries of local and subregional importance. These distinctions affected how refugees participated in local systems for gaining access to food and natural resources. Whereas for the people involved these local institutions proved successful in regulating food and accommodating tensions, certain external policies threatened to undermine these. Both refugee and host experiences differed by gender and social group.

134 **Lee, Luke T.** (1996) Internally displaced persons and refugees: toward a legal synthesis? *Journal of Refugee Studies,* 9 (1): 27-42.

"The number of internally displaced persons now exceeds that of refugees. Although both categories of people are coerced or compelled to flee their homelands in fear for life, liberty, and security, only refugees are entitled to systematic international protection and assistance under existing international treaties and instruments, which require the crossing of international borders as a prerequisite. This despite the fact that internally displaced persons often suffer more than refugees. Such a prerequisite may be challenged on historical, practical, juridical, and human rights grounds, whose validity is examined in this paper. The paper concludes with a strong plea for reconsidering the use of the crossing of international borders as a prerequisite to systematic international protection and assistance of people forcibly displaced from their homes."

135 **Leliveld, Andre** (1994) The impact of labour migration on the Swazi rural homestead as solidarity group. In K. and F. von Benda-Beckmann & H. Marks (eds) *Coping with insecurity: an 'underall' perspective on social security in the Third World.* Special Issue Focaal 22/23, pp. 177-198.

This paper examines what labour migration means to the social security role of the Swazi rural homestead. The author discusses the relationship between labour migration and the conditions which determine whether or not a social group can act as a solidarity group, and estimates the impact of labour migration on the rural homestead in its capacity as a solidarity group. Data are derived from a 1990 survey among 115 rural homesteads situated on Swazi Nation Land. The author shows that the impact of labour migration differs according to the type of homestead. As a solidarity group, homesteads in the establishment and expansion stage are far more affected by labour migration than homesteads in other stages of the developmental cycle (consolidation, fission, decline).

136 **Liebkind, Karmela** (1993) Self-reported ethnic identity, depression and anxiety among young Vietnamese refugees and their parents. *Journal of Refugee Studies,* 6 (1): 25-39.

"There are approximately 2500 Indochinese refugees in Finland dispersed in small groups throughout the country. This study assesses to what extent the young generation of refugees is moving away from the values and culture of their parents, and to what extent this creates conflicts between the generations and emotional stress. Cultural identity and emotional stress are measured with several indices. The results from the Hopkins Symptom Checklist 25 and the Vietnamese depression Scale are presented. The sample of the study consists of two generations, 159 young refugees born in 1969-1976 and 121 of their parents/caregivers. The results of the study suggest that the amount of self-reported anxiety and depression tend to increase with length of stay in Finland, in both generations. The symptom level is higher among females than males. Time in the resettlement country also clearly affects the ethnic self-perception of the youth (in the direction of more 'Finnishness'), but not that of the adults. This could produce increasing generational strain and explain the rising symptom level."

137 **Lipsky, Sherry, & Ky Nimol** (1993) Khmer Women Healers in Transition: Cultural and Bureaucratic Barriers in Training and Employment. *Journal of Refugee Studies*, 6 (4): 372-388.

"Kmer women healers and health workers in a refugee camp on the Thai-Cambodian border describe their evolving roles and status: historically, as traditional healers and midwives, to present-day employment in the formal sector in Cambodia and in the camp. The women also identify the cultural beliefs and practices which place women in the home, and taboos against working with men, resulting in restricted access to education and employment for women. These reports are supported by those of other health workers in the camp. Additionally, the numerical and role discrepancies between male and female health training graduates and workers documented in this study validate these reports: approximately 25 per cent were women, concentrated in lower level courses and positions (with the exception of midwives). The fears and expectations of repatriation for women health workers are briefly explored. Implications for program policy and planning and research, particularly for Khmer women in transition, are addressed."

138 **Lipson, Juliene G., & Suellen Miller** (1994) Changing Roles of Afghan Refugee Women in the United States. *Health Care for Women International*, 15 (3): 171-180.

Examines adjustment issues & role changes of Afghan women refugees in northern CA, drawing on interviews with 32 Afghan women. Although similar issues were expressed by most respondents, generation influenced the experience of such issues. The elderly suffer from social isolation & lack of respect; the middle generation shoulders the triple burden of housewife, employee, & mediator between children & spouse; & young & single women face culture conflict & the lack of appropriate mates. 13 References. Adapted from the source document. (Copyright 1995, Sociological Abstracts, Inc., all rights reserved.)

139 **Loescher, Gill** (1993) *Beyond charity: international cooperation and the global refugee crisis.* New York/Oxford: Oxford University Press.

This book provides a concise examination of the (international) historical context of today's refugee and asylum problem since the aftermath of WWI, and its present implications. The primary issue addressed is whether the contemporary refugee regime is capable of dealing effectively with the newly emerging international refugee crisis, the increasingly restrictive asylum and resettlement policies in the industrialised world, and the persistent poverty and instability in the South that are called upon to provide asylum. The author argues that it is no longer sufficient to respond to the refugee crisis as a strictly humanitarian problem, but that a pressing need exists for a more comprehensive political response.

140 **Lutz, Helma** (1990) Cultural/Ethnic Identity in the Safety Net of Cultural Hegemony. *European Journal of Intercultural Studies,* 1 (2): 5-13.

The new concept of cultural/ethnic identity in the social sciences – giving ethnic minorities the opportunity to act on the basis of an autonomously defined identity – is criticized for its "liberalizing" nature. Cultural/ethnic identity often simply fulfills an "alibi function" in pluralistic ideologies, leaving but a small margin for autonomous self-definition within the ideological operations of cultural domination. As a consequence, minority groups are confronted with the dilemma of having to construct an autonomous concept of cultural identity, in opposition to, but within the structures of cultural hegemony. The question is raised of whether the concept is useful & necessary for the advancement of intercultural studies. 39 References. Adapted from the source document. (Copyright 1992, Sociological Abstracts, Inc., all rights reserved.)

141 **Lutz, Helma** (1991) The Myth of the 'Other': Western Representation and Images of Migrant Women of So Called 'Islamic Background'. *Revue Internationale de Sociologie / International Review of Sociology (nouvelle serie / new series),* 2 (121-137.): -137.

Focus is on the question of the images that Western scientists have created – & still perpetuate – of migrant women from the so-called Islamic countries. An overview is given of the history of production & reproduction of "orientalization" of women. Special interest is shown in how these images are perpetuated in present paradigms within research on migrant women. A more appropriate & theoretically more constructive approach of research on migrant women is urged (Copyright 1992, Sociological Abstracts, Inc., all rights reserved.)

142 **Lutz, Helma** (1995) The Legacy of Migration: Immigrant Mothers and Daughters and the Process of Intergenerational Transmission. *Comenius,* 15 (3): 304-317.

In this biography of 2 Surinamese women, mother and daughter, living in the Netherlands, it becomes clear how immigrants use their cultural resources and intergenerational transmission of knowledge to cope with environmental changes. The mother has adapted the values of the Creole Volksklasse matrifocal family structure to contemporary Dutch society, providing her children with an excellent education and equipment to integrate, thus making them less vulnerable to discrimination. The daughter however, decides to return to Surinam, disapproving of her parents migration and confirming her roots. Through their narratives it becomes evident that continuity and change in intergenerational transmission should be studied in order to get an insight into the emotional consequences of migration.

143 **Macklin, Audrey** (1995) Refugee Women and the Imperative of Categories. *Human Rights Quarterly,* 17 (2): 213-277.

Guidelines issued by the Canadian Immigration & Refugee Board in 1993 are used to examine the theoretical & practical implications of using gender as a category in refugee determination. The intent of the guidelines was to interpret the legal definition of a refugee in a gender-sensitive manner, & may be seen as the first formal move by a state to recognize gender prosecution. The guidelines are examined in the broader context of Canadian & international refugee law. The guidelines are critiqued, noting gaps & omissions. Questions of the self/other are also seen to be part of the debate, as gender persecution in refugee acceptor countries remains an issue. A. Cole (Copyright 1995, Sociological Abstracts, Inc., all rights reserved.)

144 **Macklin, Audrey** (1996) Opening the door to women refugees: a first crack. In W. Giles, H. Moussa, & P. van Esterik (eds) *Development and diaspora: gender and the refugee experience.* Canada: Artemis Enterprises, pp. 118-142.

In this paper the author analyzes the Canadian *Guidelines on Women Refugee Claimants Fearing Gender-Related Persecution,* issued by the Immigration and Refugee Board in 1993. These guidelines form a precedent in the international arena of refugee law and asylum regulations. However, they are critiqued by the author because they are not law and thus not binding, and furthermore because they only apply to the small minority of refugee women able to reach Canada. See also: previous reference, Macklin (1995).

145 **Madzokere, Claudia** (1993) Gender and work – past, present and future: the situation of rural Mozambican women at Mozowe River Bridge Camp in Zimbabwe. *Journal of Social Development in Africa,* 8 (2): 23-32.

The author has studied some 200 Mozambican refugee women at Mazowe River Bridge Camp in Zimbabwe, comparing their roles and status before and after their displacement and projecting their future after repatriation. His data support S.T. Makanya's (1990) findings at a similar camp in that women take the major responsibility for domestic and other chores, just as in Mozambique. Men are no longer the family providers but they still make the decisions, leaving women vulnerable and dependent. This will change due to the skills women acquire in the camps but there is still a long way to go for them to be fully recognized as being able to work outside the home.

146 **Mahmud, Nasreen** (1996) Crimes against Honour: Women in International Refugee Law. *Journal of Refugee Studies,* 9 (4): 367-382.

"This article examines two perspectives concerning refugee women in the legal literature. One perspective argues that sex should be included in the Convention definition as a persecutory ground and that the concept of 'persecution' itself should be reformulated to incorporate the experience of women. The second perspective argues that a distinction must be drawn between persecutory form and a persecutory ground, and that issues relating to sex can be better addressed within the legal structures which currently exist. The article first provides a backdrop to the debate which discusses sexual violence and other forms of violence against women which exist in the refugee context; then gives a detailed exposition of both perspectives; discuss the issues in a practical sense with reference to the Canadian experience; and finally provides comparisons and conclusions."

ANNOTATED BIBLIOGRAPHY   133

147 **Majka, Lorraine, & Brendan Mullan** (1992) Employment Retention, Area of Origin, and Type of Social Support among Refugees in the Chicago Area. *International Migration Review,* 26 (3[99]): 899-926.

"This article examines the impact of various sociodemographic variables on refugees' employment propensities in the greater metropolitan Chicago area. It extends existing research and knowledge of forced migrants' labor force activities by exploring the impact of region of origin and refugees' access to support systems and organizations on employment retention and job maintenance. The analysis shows that refugees' labor force participation patterns and experiences are influenced differentially both by their background characteristics and by their exposure to US assistance systems. Southeast Asian asylees are less successful maintaining stable job placements when compared to their more socially advantaged and often more suitably placed Eastern European counterparts. Refugee self-help initiatives require greater empowerment and increased acceptance and status to assist other refugees in adjusting to the host society."

148 **Malkki, Liisa H.** (1994) Citizens of Humanity: Internationalism and the Imagined Community of Nations. *Diaspora,* 3 (1): 41-68.

Explores the processes & practices that allow the contemporary system of nation-states to be imagined as a global community, as a family of nations. Following a brief description of a 1964 Bob Hope film, The Global Affair, is a discussion of how Hutu refugees from Burundi living in a refugee camp in western Tanzania imagined the international community at a particular time (1958/86) & why they attached such importance to it. This startling juxtaposition shows that key forms in the political imagination of international order are shared globally, & that these forms can take on profoundly different meanings & uses, depending on the local sociopolitical context. Additional examples of the transnational imagining of nation-states as a world community included amusement park rides, travel writing, pornography, ethnologies, children's games, beauty pageants, & the Olympic games. 67 References. M. Maguire (Copyright 1996, Sociological Abstracts, Inc., all rights reserved.)

149 **Malkki, Liisa H.** (1995) Refugees and Exile: From "Refugee Studies" to the National Order of Things. *Annual Review of Anthropology,* 24 (495-523): -523.

"This review offers a critical mapping of the construction-in-progress of refugees and displacement as an anthropological domain of knowledge. It situates the emergence of 'the refugee' and of 'refugee studies' in two ways: first, historically, by looking at the management of displacement in Europe in the wake of World War II; and second, by tracing an array of different discursive and institutional domains within which 'the refugee' and /or 'being in exile' have been constituted. These domains include international law, international studies, documentary production by the United Nations and other international refugee agencies, development studies, and literary studies. The last part of the review briefly discusses recent work on displacement diaspora, and deterritorialization in the context of studies of cultural identity, nationalism, transnational cultural forms – work that helps to conceptualize the anthropological study of displacement in new ways."

150 **Malkki, Liisa H.** (1995) *Purity and exile: violence, memory, and national cosmology among Hutu refugees in Tanzania.* Chicago/London: University of Chicago Press.

In this study the author concerns herself with an exploration of how displacement and deterritorialization – conditions that seem 'normal' for more and more people today – shape the social construction of 'nationness' and history, identity and enmity. This is done through a study of Hutu refugees who fled the massacres in Burundi in 1972 and found asylum in Tanzania. The author compares the experiences and conceptualizations of self-settled Hutu refugees in a Tanzanian town with those of Hutus in the camp. The latter adhered to a strong sense of collective identity whereas the town refugees seemed to 'move through' identity categories more easily, which to them meant a means of freedom and security.

151 **Malkki, Liisa H.** (1996) Speechless Emissaries: Refugees, Humanitarianism, and Dehistoricization. *Cultural Anthropology,* 11 (3): 377-404.

Explores the forms taken by humanitarian interventions in the plight of refugees, drawing on fieldwork conducted with Burundi Hutu refugees living in Tanzania since 1972. It is noted that refugees formed different understandings of their status depending on whether they lived in camps or towns, indicating that the sense of refugee identity is contingent on historical & political contexts. In contrast, humanitarian administrators in Tanzania are demonstrated to imagine an ideal refugee identity against which actual refugees are constantly compared & judged. The vision that animates administrators' sense of the ideal refugee is shown to consist of images of raw human need in a state of minimal humanity. It is argued that this vision tends to silence & trivialize history & politics & thus ignore broad aspects of the refugee experience. The consequences of this vision are discussed in relation to the 1994 genocide in Rwanda. A call is made to historicize & politicize the humanism that guides the administration of humanitarian relief for refugees. 66 References. D. M. Smith (Copyright 1997, Sociological Abstracts, Inc., all rights reserved.)

152 **Markowitz, Fran** (1994) Responding to events from afar: Soviet Jewish refugees reassess their identity. In L.A. Camino & R.M. Krulfeld (eds) *Reconstructing lives, recapturing meaning: refugee identity, gender and culture change.* Washington D.C.: Gordon and Breach Publishers, pp. 57-69.

This paper explores culture change and adaptation among refugee communities through a study of Russo-Soviet Jews who have been resettled in the United States and Israel since the 1970s and early 1980s. For these refugees, their identity includes an emphasis on the suffering and hardship endured during the adjustment to their new environments. The paper further examines the differential interpretation of shared ethnicity by focusing on the interaction between these refugees and the new cohort of Soviet refugees arriving in the 1990s. Due to a confrontation with the new refugees who are now the 'other', the older resettled refugees have to re-examine themselves, and reassess their identities as Russian refugees in the West.

153 **Markowitz, Fran** (1996) Living in Limbo: Bosnian Muslim Refugees in Israel. *Human Organization,* 55 (2): 127-132.

This paper gives data obtained through field observations and interviews in 1993/94 with 71 Bosnian Muslim families in Israel.They maintain family cohesion and their ethno-national identity while in limbo. This situation is relatively secure and stable and since Israeli government policy is family- and work-oriented Bosnian family heads can provide for their children and maintain gender complementarity within the household. Instead of forcing long term commitment to a new country this policy may prevent cultural clashes and social problems.

154 **Marsella, A. et al. (eds)** (1992) *Amidst peril and pain: understanding the mental health and wellbeing of the world's refugees.* Washington D.C.: American Psychological Association Press.

"This multidisciplinary volume provides an overview of refugee mental health problems and suggests approaches to intervention. It is impossible to isolate these problems from the context in which they arise, and as a result the book also provides information on demographics, history, epidemiology, policy formation, mental health services, training, and specific regional concerns. The book is divided into five parts including an up-to-date overview of the current crisis and historical background; information on populations in specific regions including Central America, Israel, the Middle East, and Southeast Asia; a discussion of the special mental health and adjustment problems of refugees; and finally, research recommendations and future goals."

155 **Marsella, Anthony J., & Alice Scheuer** (1993) Coping: Definitions, Conceptualizations, and Issues. *Integrative Psychiatry,* 9 (3-4): 124-134.

The emergence & evolution of coping as a popular theoretical & research topic is traced through a historical review of the literature & examples of definitions. A new definition of coping is offered that includes major dimensions of previous definitions. The literature on coping resources (ie, personality & social) & coping behaviors (ie, beliefs, attitudes, thinking styles, action behaviors) is reviewed. An evolutionary model of human growth & development is proposed in which coping occupies the pivotal space between behaviors (eg, reflexes, defenses) – characterized by stasis, inefficiency, distress, & fragmentation – & behaviors (eg, coping, competency) – characterized by becoming, efficiency, well-being, & integration. 2 Figures, 88 References. Adapted from the source document. (Copyright 1995, Sociological Abstracts, Inc., all rights reserved.)

156 **Martin, Lila M.** (1998) *Female Genital Mutilation: A Claim for Asylum Based on Gender Persecution.* Association Paper.

Examines traditional US Immigration & Naturalization Services law as it pertains to refugees, arguing that the adjudication of asylum case law has been largely determined by the experiences of men, & women's rights have been uniformly excluded from human rights discourse. However, following Canada's example, the US now recognizes gender-related persecution, eg, female genital mutilation, as a valid claim for asylum. The need for the UN to recognize gender-based persecution by adding gender as a sixth category to its definition of a refugee is reiterated. This step will give women's experiences recognition equal to that given the other five categories of political persecution: race, ethnicity, religion, membership in a particular social group, & political opinion. (Copyright 1998, Sociological Abstracts, Inc., all rights reserved.)

157 **Martin, Susan F., & Emily Copeland** (1988) Making Ends Meet?: Refugee Women and Income Generation. *Humboldt Journal of Social Relations*, 15 (2): 29-91.

The author examines income generation projects and other ways to help refugee women to increase their financial resources. The programs have considerably improved their economic well-being, but have reached few needy households and have focused on a narrow range of economic activities. Suggestions are made to improve efforts to increase self-sufficiency of refugee women.

158 **Mazur, Robert E.** (1989) The political economy of refugee creation in Southern Africa: micro and macro issues in sociological perspective. *Journal of Refugee Studies*, 2 (4): 441-467.

"Causes, conditions and consequences of displacement in Southern Africa are examined. A political economy framework is introduced and modified to incorporate regional issues and 'destabilization', or low-intensity conflict. Within this framework, micro and macro sociological issues concerning refugees and displaced persons are explicitly linked. Special emphasis is placed on sociological processes crucial for rebuilding individual lives, families, communities and nations in Southern Africa and elsewhere. The role of the international community in this problem and possible solutions are discussed."

159 **McCallin, Margaret (ed)** (1996) *The psychological well-being of refugee children: research, practice and policy issues.* Geneva: ICCB.

This publication consists of the revised papers given at a seminar convened by the International Catholic Child Bureau in 1991. The seminar focused on raising awareness and understanding of the multiple factors that influence the psychological well-being of refugee children and their families. The different papers explicitly deal with policy issues and strategies that can enhance the psychological well-being of refugee children. Includes twenty-five separate papers.

160 **McSpadden, Lucia A.** (1987) Ethiopian Refugee Resettlement in the Western United States: Social Context and Psychological Well-Being. *International Migration Review*, 21 (3): 796-819.

The psychological well-being of M Ethiopian refugees in Calif, Wash, & Nev is investigated via questionnaire, scale, & interview data (N = 59). Results indicate that the level of stress among Ethiopian refugees resettled by agencies is higher than that of those resettled by volunteers. When English-speaking ability is held constant, the differential ability of these two resettlement methodologies to provide appropriate employment & access to higher education varies directly with stress levels. Recommendations for improvements are offered. 5 Tables, 15 References. Modified HA (Copyright 1988, Sociological Abstracts, Inc., all rights reserved.)

161 **McSpadden, Lucia A., & Helene Moussa** (1993) I Have a Name: The Gender Dynamics in Asylum and in Resettlement of Ethiopian and Eritrean Refugees in North America. *Journal of Refugee Studies,* 6 (3): 203-225.

"Two independent studies of Ethiopian / Eritrean refugees, one of single men and one of women, are used to compare and contrast the particularities of the refugee experience for women and men. The clearly differentiated gender identities of the home culture were seen to affect the subjects' attempts to rebuild their lives and reconstruct their identity in the new environment. The status of men in the home culture being higher, they found it difficult to come to terms with a lower status and limited opportunities on resettlement. Women, in contrast, had already experienced a conflict in the home environment between their traditional and their individual aspirations. In addition, the traumatic experiences in flight and asylum (such as rape, and the possibility of prostitution as the only survival strategy) made the women realize that for them, there was a much lower status than 'menial' employment. Consequently, they tended to see the new environment as offering more possibilities for them in the long term, and to have less difficulty in accepting a low position in the short term."

162 **Menjivar, Cecilia** (1993) History, economy and politics: macro and micro-level factors in recent Salvadorean migration to the US. *Journal of Refugee Studies,* 6 (4): 350-371.

"Through an analysis at the macro and micro levels, this study argues that the root cause of Salvadorean migration during the 1980s has been an interplay between economic and political factors. The analysis of this proposition at the macro level includes an examination of key political decisions that intertwined with economic policies in Salvadorean history leading to the events within which massive Salvadorean emigration unfolded. Evaluation at the individual level is based on data gathered through fieldwork conducted in California from 1989 to 1992. These sources of data include a survey of 150 Salvadorean men and women of whom 40 were selected for intensive interviews. The main conclusion of this study is that the conjecture

ANNOTATED BIBLIOGRAPHY 139

of the political and the economic, at the macro and micro levels, shapes the motivation to leave, making it analytically difficult to separate the two. Furthermore, certain conditioning socio-demographic characteristics, such as education, gender, and age, interact in specific ways with broader forces in the politico-economic framework to affect individual desires and motives. A recommendation for future work on this problem is to include the voices and experiences of those who participate in refugee migrations, in order to make more accurate statements about the effects of broader forces on the lives of these migrants."

163 **Meznaric, Silva** (1994) Gender as an ethno-marker: rape, war and identity politics in the former Yugoslavia. In V.M. Moghadam (ed) *Identity politics & women: cultural reassertions and feminisms in international perspective.* Boulder/San Francisco/Oxford: Westview Press, pp. 76-97.

In this chapter the author examines two cases wherein women and their bodies have been pawns in male directed battles over ethnic identity. She shows how rape as politics in the Serbian aggression in Bosnia (1992-3) has roots in the Kosovo conflict of the late 1980s. In both cases gender, ethnic identity and political competition intersected, with tragic consequences. The main argument of this chapter is that gender serves as an ethno-marker in boundary maintenance and in conflicts between groups.

164 **Miserez, Diana** (1995) *Faith, hope and courage: the great strengths of refugees.* London: Adelphi Press.

In this book the author, who has been actively engaged in refugee work over the past thirty years, portrays the different refugee crisis of these decades, and their historical antecedents, with special emphasis on the refugees' experiences. From the many case stories described, the strength and vitality of refugees becomes evident, as well as their contributions to receiving societies.

165 **Moghadam, Valentine M. (ed)** (1994) *Identity politics and women: cultural reassertions and feminisms in international perspective.* Boulder CO/ Oxford: Westview Press.

Identity politics refers to discourses and movements organised around questions of religious, ethnic and national identity. The papers in this volume particularly explore the relations of culture, identity and women by means of diverse case studies that show the nature of 'Woman' as cultural symbol and 'Woman' as political pawn in male-dominated and male-directed power struggles. At the same time, these case studies provide evidence of women as active participants and opponents of such conceptualisations and movements. Individual papers are subsumed under three headings: theoretical, comparative and historical perspectives; country case studies; dilemmas and strategies.

166 **Mohamed Salih, M.A.** (1996) Responding to situations of mass voluntary return: past experience in Sudan. In T. Allen (ed) *In search of cool ground : war, flight & homecoming in northeast Africa.* London: James Currey, pp. 164-170.

This paper discusses one of the first and largest assisted mass voluntary return operations that took place in Sudan after the Addis Ababa Agreement of 1972. During the foregoing civil war about a million people had fled their home areas, of whom about 200,000 fled to neighbouring countries. 'Rehabilitation' required not only the rebuilding of what had once existed, but in many respects actually initiating the development process. The author describes how this difficult return operation turned out to be successful because the Sudanese government was in a position to link relief and development. This was due to the fact that an attempted communist coup in Sudan made the major aid donor countries very willing to help, and furthermore it was in the political interest of Nimeiri's government in Khartoum to end the war and encourage foreign investment.

167 **Monzel, Kristen** (1993) 'Only the women know': powerlessness and marginality in three Hmong women's lives. In R. Black & V. Robinson (eds) *Geography and refugees: patterns and processes of change.* London/New York: Belhaven Press, pp. 118-133.

In this paper the author presents the experiences and life stories of three Hmong women, with the aim of highlighting what it means and how it feels to be a refugee. The main theme in these stories is the lack of control over personal matters, over war, and over 'a place called home'. The author concludes that these gendered experiences show how refugee women are even more marginalised and powerless than refugee men, and argues in favour of a correction of Western-biased and male-biased assumptions about forced migration.

168 Moore, Lisa (1993) Among Khmer and Vietnamese refugee women in Thailand: no safe place. In D. Bell, P. Caplan, & W.J. Karim (eds) *Gendered fields: women, men and ethnography.* London/New York: Routledge, pp. 117-127.

The book in which this paper is published explores issues concerning gender and fieldwork from within the framework of recent feminist and postmodernist debates. In her paper the author tells of her experiences of doing research in refugee camps on the Thai – Cambodian border. One main subject is the author's feeling of vulnerability to rape and assault as a female researcher in the lawless environment of the camps. During her fieldwork, and as a consequence of her daily contact with the refugee women, the author explores her own selfhood. This involves questions of individuality versus belonging as well as the contradiction felt between being a representative of the dominant power in the region (i.e. American), while at the same time being vulnerable like all women.

169 Moors, Annelies et al. (1990) *Refugee and displaced women.* Leiden: VENA, Leiden University.

"This issue of the VENA Newsletter is devoted to discussions about refugee women. Most of the discussions focus on international relief and assistance programmes, refugee relief, gender sensitive planning, the needs and priorities of refugee women in development, protection issues, and women's participation in programme development and the research process. Specific articles focus on Palestinian women in exile, refugee women in the Netherlands, gender sensitive development planning in the refugee context and Eritrean refugee women in Eastern Sudan." (taken from Neuwirth & Vincent [1997])

170 Mortland, Carol A., & Judy Ledgerwood (1987) Secondary Migration among Southeast Asian Refugees in the United States. *Urban Anthropology,* 16 (3-4): 291-326.

Since the beginning of the resettlement of Southeast Asian refugees to the US in 1975, the movement of refugees away from their initial placement locality has become a concern for government & resettlement agencies who worry about refugees' loss of sponsors & the consequences that result from large refugee concentrations in urban areas. Viewing secondary migration from an anthropological perspective reveals that it is part of a larger process: it is a voluntary act by the refugee that is profoundly influenced by traditional kinship relationships, patronage systems, & Southeast Asian mobility. Such a perspective permits a greater understanding of Southeast Asian refugee mobility in the US, & the obstacles facing those who attempt to prevent it. 92 References. Modified HA (Copyright 1988, Sociological Abstracts, Inc., all rights reserved.)

171 **Mortland, Carol A.** (1994) Cambodian refugees and identity in the United States. In L.A. Camino & R.M. Krulfeld (eds) *Reconstructing lives, recapturing meaning: refugee identity, gender and culture change.* Washington D.C.: Gordon and Breach Publishers, pp. 5-28.

This paper deals with the interrelations between ethnic and refugee identity through a discussion of Cambodian identity among Khmer who fled the Khmer Rouge genocide of the Pol Pot regime and who now reside in the United States. The author finds that 'Cambodianness' and 'refugeeness' cannot be reckoned without respect to one another, and shows how being Cambodian has been converted by this group of refugees into concepts that include references to survivorhood, suffering, pain and loss. At the same time, there is much pride in being a refugee from Cambodia, as this implies carrying forth the ancient Angkor civilization. The author delineates four contextual domains used by the Cambodian refugees to conceptualize their identity, and argues that identification with these different domains is situational, dependent on the particular and changing circumstances of social interaction.

172 **Moussa, Helene** (1993) *Storm and sanctuary: the journey of European and Eritrean women refugees.* Ontario: Artemis Enterprises.

This book examines the discontinuities and continuities in the lives of Ethiopian and Eritrean women refugees who fled their country during the military dictatorship of Mengistu (1974-1991) and resettled in Canada. Life histories are used as the methodological tool to identify how these women made meaning of their lives in a new environment, trying to continue their personal life goals. The analysis of their experiences reveals how refugee women, in their search to belong, struggle to reconstruct their identities. The author concludes that the refugee experience in many cases is a source of strength, and that refugee women are subjects rather than objects of their future.

173 **Moussa, Helene** (1995) Caught between two worlds: Eritrean women refugees and voluntary repatriation. In Sorenson (ed) *Disaster and development in the Horn of Africa.* UK: Macmillan Press Ltd.

This paper deals with issues of return in the lives of Eritrean women refugees. It shows their dilemmas in deciding whether or not to return back home after having rebuilt and reshaped their lives in exile. Gender issues and issues of belonging and identity play a part. The author suggests that the new strength and resilience that many of the Eritrean women built in exile, may prove powerful resources for their reestablishment and reintegration into the (changed) Eritrean society.

174 **Muecke, Marjorie A.** (1992) New Paradigms for Refugee Health Problems. *Social Science and Medicine,* 35 (4): 515-523.

A critique is offered of two paradigms that have shaped the understanding of refugee health: the objectification of refugees as a political class of excess people, & the reduction of refugee health to disease or pathology. Then, alternative paradigms are recommended that consider the polyvocality of refugees & construe them as prototypes of resilience despite major losses & stressors. Secondary research is drawn on to trace the life history of refugees from internal displacement in the country of origin, to asylum in a second (usually neighboring) country, & for some, to permanent resettlement in a third country. Primary topics in the literature on refugee health are identified, along with key problems for further research. 97 References. Adapted from the source document. (Copyright 1993, Sociological Abstracts, Inc., all rights reserved.)

175 **Neuwirth, Gertrud, & Christine Vincent (eds)** (1997) *Women refugees in international perspectives 1980-1990: an annotated bibliography.* Ontario, Canada: RRDR.

This annotated bibliography is a compendium volume to the original *Refugee women: selected and annotated bibliography* (1985), its revised 1989 edition, and the 'Select bibliography' in Special Issues on Refugee Women in *Refugee Survey Quarterly,* vol. 14, 1985, all published by the UNHCR Centre for Documentation on Refugees. In the current bibliography compiled by the Research Resource Division for Refugees, Carleton University, Canada, references are subsumed under the following headings: general concerns; country of origin conditions; asylum; countries of resettlement; health, mental health and health care; social and cultural issues.

176 **Oliver-Smith, Anthony** (1991) Involuntary resettlement, resistance and political empowerment. *Journal of Refugee Studies,* 4 (2): 132-149.

"The nature of resistance to resettlement is examined through a discussion of cognitive aspects as well as factors influencing or evoking resistance movements. Resettlement resistance movements vary according to strategies adopted either to resist resettlement implementation or to gain bargaining advantage for improving resettlement projects. The array of tactics which people have employed to resist resettlement is broad, including legal and illegal and non-violent and violent measures. One important consideration which emerges from this examination is the expansion of resistance to resettlement into more generalized forms of empowerment. Three cases of failed resistance, which nonetheless led to increased local empowerment, are briefly explored."

177 **Oloka-Onyango, Joe** (1996) The plight of the larger half: human rights, gender violence and the legal status of refugee and internally displaced women in Africa. *Denver Journal International Law and Policy,* 24 (2/3): 349-394.

In this paper the author inquires the nature of insecurity experienced by refugee women and by doing so sets a framework for a critique of international and regional law concerned with refugees. One of the guiding questions is why international law in general is so oblivious to the overall situation of women. Furthermore, the author addresses the issue of whether feminist critiques of the international arena are in fact sensitive to the conditions of African women. Secondly this paper is concerned with the place of gender in the main refugee instruments. The latter inquiry is linked to human rights law and the operations of the UNHCR.

178 **Omidian, Patricia A.** (1993) Afghan refugee males: betwixt and between. In Nieto & Rainey (eds) *Under fire: voices of minority males, vol.1.* pp. 107-116.

"In this paper case studies of Afghan refugee males will be used to illustrate key issues in community mental health and how these issues affect the males of the community. These issues – including role and status loss, role reversal, and PTSD – are applicable to other immigrant and refugee populations, because the plight of the Afghan refugee is not particularly unique. Data were based on research in a California refugee community and were gathered over the course of nine years."

179 Ong, Aihwa, Virginia R. Dominguez, Jonathan Friedman, Nina G. Schiller, V. Stolcke, David Y.H. Wu, & Hu Ying (1996) Cultural Citizenship as Subject-Making: Immigrants Negotiate Racial and Cultural Boundaries in the United States. *Current Anthropology*, 37 (5): 737-751.

Cultural citizenship is examined as a process of subjectification through ethnographic analysis of the citizenship-making experiences of two Asian immigrant groups in the US from different class backgrounds: poor Cambodian refugees & affluent Chinese cosmopolitans. Analysis reveals that institutional practices differentiate between Asian immigrants on the basis of gender, position within racial hierarchies, class, & consumption; & immigrants must daily negotiate lines of difference in state & civil society. Comments are offered by Virginia R. Dominguez, Jonathan Friedman, Nina Glick Schiller, Verena Stolcke, David Y. H. Wu, & Hu Ying. In her Reply, Ong responds to each of the commentators, emphasizing issues of imputation of racializing processes, the comparative anthropology of racism, the role of nationalism in citizen making, & empowerment of Asian immigrant groups. 100 References. Adapted from the source document. (Copyright 1997, Sociological Abstracts, Inc., all rights reserved.)

180 Opondo, Enoch O. (1996) Refugee repatriation in the Horn of Africa : a contextual overview of some socio-economic, legal & administrative constraints. In T. Allen (ed) *In search of cool ground : war, flight & homecoming in northeast Africa.* London: James Currey, pp. 23-34.

This paper highlights the complexity of forced migration in the Horn of Africa, arguing that the process of flight in this region has almost become indistinguishable from the process of return. The author distinguishes two main reasons for voluntary return movements: first, the continuation of socioeconomic and political problems in the region which often make conditions in the host societies similarly bad to that which the refugees escaped from; and second, the inability of the international humanitarian and refugee assistance regime to live up to the objectives of protecting refugees and promoting their voluntary repatriation, or resettlement and assimilation elsewhere. The author identifies weaknesses in the existing refugee assistance regime and gives some suggestions as to why these need to be guarded against in the Horn's repatriation processes.

181 **Palmer, Celia** (1998) Women, health and humanitarian aid in conflict. *Disasters,* 22 (3): 236-249.

The burden of political conflict on civilian populations has increased significantly over the last decades. Increasingly, the provision of resources and services to these populations is coming under scrutiny; we highlighted here the limited attention to gender in their provision. Women and men have different exposures to situations that affect health and access to health care and have differential power to influence decisions regarding the provision of health services. We argue that the role of women in planning is central to the provision of effective, efficient and sensitive health care to affected populations.

182 **PANOS** (1995) *Arms to fight, arms to protect: women speak about conflict.* London: PANOS.

This book holds the non-uniform experiences of women in situations of conflict and war. Their testimonies reveal the views and experiences of women as fighters, participants, refugees, victims, organisers for peace and rehabilitation, carers, and mothers, relatives and partners of the dead and disappeared. Women from four continents speak of how they deal with the psychological and physical damage of war as well as with economic survival. The dominant impression from the testimonies is one of individuals surviving with strength and ingenuity.

183 **Parker, Melissa** (1996) Social devastation & mental health in northeast Africa : some reflections on an absent literature. In T. Allen (ed) *In search of cool ground : war, flight & homecoming in northeast Africa.* London: James Currey, pp. 262-273.

This paper discusses the limited attempts by psychiatrists and psychoanalysts to document the longer term consequences of war among non-Western populations in clinical settings. Furthermore, the psychiatric and psychoanalytic literature that is available, mostly assumes a mind/body dualism and a notion of self that is inextricably intertwined with Western notions of autonomy and individual responsibility. Research shows, however, that health, illness and the notion of self for example, are culturally constructed in many different ways. The author concludes that, in spite of the cultural bias in the Western understanding of trauma, some of its ideas may be helpful in the North African context. However, much is still unclear as to what exactly the benefits may be of applying these ideas and concepts to refugees.

ANNOTATED BIBLIOGRAPHY

184 **Partnoy, Alicia (ed)** (1987) *You can't drown the fire: Latin American women writing in exile.* Pittsburg, San Francisco: Cleis Press.

This volume holds the writings, personal accounts and life stories narrated by Latin American women who have been living in exile for different political, social and economic reasons and in different parts of the world. It portrays their suffering as well as their ingeneous dealings with the dilemmas of life in exile.

185 **Quack, Sybille (ed)** (1995) *Between sorrow and strength: women refugees of the Nazi period.* Washington D.C.: German Historical Institute.

Refugees of the Nazi period have attracted considerable attention from scholars. This volume, which intends to show how refugee women endured during the Nazi period, underscores their important role in the survival of their families, and explores the meaning that exile and emigration had for their future lives and careers. Included are papers by noted scholars in the field as well as eyewitness reports from contemporaries who relate their actual experiences. This combination of sources reveals a gender perspective on the history of Jewish as well as non-Jewish emigration from Europe during the Nazi era.

186 **Rapone, Anita, & Charles R. Simpson** (1996) Women's Response to Violence in Guatemala: Resistance and Rebuilding. *International Journal of Politics, Culture and Society,* 10 (1): 115-140.

Discusses responses of two groups of women to the violent repressive strategies of the Guatemalan government in the 1970s & 1980s: women involved in human rights organizations in urban & military rural communities, & women in refugee camps. Government strategies included violence against individuals deemed hostile to the state, attacks on demonstrations & offices of popular organizations, & the use of massive military power against rebels & peasant communities. In the face of this violence, women in human rights organizations organized the Grupo de Apoyo Mutuo, an organization of families of the disappeared, & the Coordinadora Nacional de Viudas de Guatemala, an organization of indigenous rural women who lost their husbands to violence. Women in refugee camps in Mexico took part in the Permanent Commissions to negotiate their return to Guatemala. This activity included training women in various camp communities to assist in food production, family planning, health care, & literacy & numeracy. An important element in the success of these activists was their ability to link their identities as women to a contested historical pro-

148   REFUGEES, GENDER AND HUMAN SECURITY

ject. D. M. Smith (Copyright 1997, Sociological Abstracts, Inc., all rights reserved.)

187 **Razack, Sherene** (1996) The perils of storytelling for refugee women. In W. Giles, H. Moussa, & P. van Esterik (eds) *Development and diaspora: gender and the refugee experience.* Canada: Artemis Enterprises, pp. 164-174.

This paper intends to examine the risks of storytelling in legal settings. The main part of the paper is a discussion of how the author saw these risks a few years ago. She then wrote a paper called *Storytelling for social change,* in which she argued that when certain groups talk about their cultures, they are heard by dominant groups in ways that make their communities seem inferior or pathological. The second part of the paper deals explicitly with the risks of storytelling for refugee women telling their stories to save their lives. Issues of multiple identities constructed in the refugee hearing, and of power differentials between listener and storyteller are discussed.

188 **Richmond, Anthony H.** (1993) Reactive Migration: Sociological Perspectives on Refugee Movements. *Journal of Refugee Studies,* 6 (1): 7-24.

"Sociological theories of migration and refugee movements are reviewed and revised in light of recent developments in structuration theory. Specifically, the dichotomy between 'voluntary' and 'involuntary' or forced migration is replaced by a continuum between *proactive* and *reactive* migration. A systems model is proposed that identifies predisposing factors, structural constraints, precipitating events, enabling circumstances and system feedback. A multivariate typology of reactive migration is described and some policy conclusions drawn."

189 **Richmond, Anthony H.** (1994) *Global apartheid: refugees, racism and the new world order.* Toronto: Oxford University Press.

In this volume the author brings together issues of migration, racism, nationalism and ethnicity in the context of globalisation. The first part of the book deals with sociological theory in debates about power, structure and agency. In this the author draws upon and reworks his earlier articles (see previous ref. Richmond 1993). His main theme is to refigure the inadequate dichotomy between voluntary and involuntary movement into a more appropriate and workable framework, for which he uses the terms proactive and reactive migration. Part two of the volume deals with migration issues as played out in the receiving societies: ethnicity, racism and multiculturalism. In part three, migration is put into the context of the post-1990 'New World Order', focusing on 'global apartheid' in terms of the increasing closure of international borders, and the concomitant control and exclusion of migrants and refugees.

190 **Rynearson, Ann M., & Pamela A. DeVoe** (1984) Refugee Women in a Vertical Village: Lowland Laotians in St. Louis. *Social Thought,* 10 (3): 33-48.

This is a case study of an apartment building in central St. Louis, Mo, with a high proportion of women among the 122 lowland Laotians occupying 32 of the 96 apartments. It concentrates on the role of women in their community structures, which shows elaborate mutual aid systems such as food exchange, resembling the situation in their homeland. Women play significant roles in ceremonies, in particular in the preparation of food. In general both sexes perform many tasks, including child care and women are encouraged to perform economic activities, which is line with their traditional custom. It is concluded that the presence of women is crucial to community functioning.

191 **Salamone, Stephen D.** (1987) Tradition and Gender: The Nikokyrio: The Economics of Sex Role Complementarity in Rural Greece. *Ethos,* 15 (2): 203-225.

A case study of the Turkish refugee community of Ammouliani, Greece, demonstrating how traditional M & F marriage roles are readapted to new socioeconomic circumstances. Described is the ideal of *nikokyra* (self-sufficient household), which has traditionally formed a framework for complementary marriage partnerships, the basic economic unit of a subsistence-based economy. It is concluded that a microanalysis of how community and communal traditions sustain the aspirations of men and women is essential to any macroanalysis of socioeconomic factors.

192 **Sayigh, Rosemary** (1981) Encounters with Palestinian Women under Occupation. *Journal of Palestine Studies,* 10 (4[40]): 3-26.

The issue of women's rights in Palestine has occasioned much interest from the media, researchers, & women's rights advocates in other countries. However, the General Union of Palestinian Women has insisted on the importance of nationalist issues over women's issues, & women in occupied Palestine engage in political protest & resistance at a significant level, as data on the arrests of about 1,400 women show. Interviews & meetings with local women leaders, intellectuals, & those occupying more traditional roles in occupied Palestine are described, illustrating the problems of the manipulation of family relationships by Israeli occupiers, & the greater role taken by women in social work capacities, especially resulting from the increasing educational opportunities for Palestinian women. However, discrimination among women has increased as a result of the educational levels attained by some of them. While all the women interviewed showed an equal commitment to Palestinian goals, less educated women were observed to suffer greater psychological strain from the occupation. D. Dunseath (Copyright 1982, Sociological Abstracts, Inc., all rights reserved.)

193 **Sayigh, Rosemary** (1988) Palestinians in Lebanon: Status Ambiguity, Insecurity and Flux. *Race and Class,* 30 (1): 13-32.

The social & political position of Palestinian refugees in Lebanon is analyzed from a historical perspective. The flight of 100,000 Palestinians into Lebanon after the Arab/Israeli war of 1948 was expected to be temporary by both the refugees & their hosts. During 1948-1969, the Palestinians met with a relatively warm reception from the Lebanon state. However, the inability of the state to wholly control the refugee population permitted, between 1969 & 1982, the emergence of the Palestinian Resistance Movement (PRM) as a power center, which polarized the Lebanese into anti- & pro-Palestinian segments. Since the 1982 Israeli invasion & PRM withdrawal, the Palestinians have faced a greater lack of security. Their place in the Lebanese economy is traced historically, & the effect of their economic status on various segments of the Lebanese population is described. A. Waters (Copyright 1989, Sociological Abstracts, Inc., all rights reserved.)

194 **Schrijvers, Joke** (1997) Internal refugees in Sri Lanka: the interplay of ethnicity and gender. *European Journal of Development Research,* 9 (2): 62-82.

"This article focuses on internal refugees in camps in Colombo in 1993. State policies have increased their dependency, a condition which is aggravated by forced resettlement programmes. Rather than reducing conflict, the policies pursued have fuelled ethnic polarisation. Although 'institutionalised' by the state and extremely dependent and vulnerable, most internal refugees are not passive victims but survivors who tried to regain some control of their lives. The interaction of ethnicity and gender appeared to be crucial constructs in their daily struggle to recapture a sense of human identity and dignity. Men in particular reacted by stressing ethnicity as the core of their identity, which was marked by gender attributes. The anthropological research methodology adopted aimed to capture the experiences and views of the refugees themselves; views which seriously questioned official state discourse."

195 **Schrijvers, Joke** (1998) Dining with the devil. Internal refugees and the nature of humanitarian aid: a case from Sri Lanka. *Forthcoming.*

During the past decade the nature of forced migration has changed, and the debate on the type of aid that should be provided to refugees has taken a new turn. During the last decade, pleas to create a more human response to refugee needs in the South, and to aim at an integration of relief and development aid, have become stronger. Recently, however, a backlash has occurred in the thinking on humanitarian aid, with strong calls for taking a far more neutral stand, reducing it to sheer emergency relief. Against the background of these debates, this article focuses on aid to internally displaced people in Sri Lanka. The main question is whether it is possible, practically as well as morally, to maintain the ideal of integrating relief and development when working with such internal refugees. The stand is taken that 'dining with the devil' and getting dirty hands seems to be unavoidable when working with internal refugees while the civil war in the country is going on. The idea that humanitarian aid should be given in a neutral way may sound convincing, but 'neutrality' in the context of violent conflicts between parties that differ substantially in power is a tricky assumption. More often than not 'neutrality' supports the more powerful parties, and their interests as a rule do not reflect the needs of politically vulnerable people such as internal refugees. It is argued therefore that the provision of humanitarian aid should continue to aim at integrating relief and people's rights to participation, self-reliance and equity, i.e. development.

196 **Scott-Villiers, Alastair, Patta Scott-Villiers, & Cole Dodge** (1993) Repatriation of 150,000 Sudanese refugees from Ethiopia: the manipulation of civilians in a situation of civil conflict. *Disasters,* 17 (3): 202-217.

"This paper outlines the dramatic return to Sudan of 150,000 men, women and children from Itang Refugee Camp in Ethiopia in June 1991. These people were pawns in Sudan's civil war, manipulated by governments, military forces and the media – a state of affairs that the international community failed to deal with effectively. At the time of the return to Sudan, ICRC and the United Nations were working to assist the returnees in two different areas and each had a different access agreement and thus a different impact on the survival of the returnees. The paper focuses on the role of political awareness and negotiation in the protection of refugees and in the organisation of relief in the context of a civil war."

197 **Scudder, T.** (1993) Development-induced relocation and refugee studies: 37 years of change and continuity among Zambia's Gwembe Tonga. *Journal of Refugee Studies,* 6 (2): 123-152.

"Development-induced, involuntary community relocation provides an exceptional opportunity for longitudinal research since 'benchmark' studies can be made before removal occurs. Because such relocation all too frequently creates development refugees, a programme of comparative long-term studies might also provide valuable knowledge for policy-makers dealing with a wider range of refugees. This possibility is explored by analysis of change and continuity among Zambia's Gwembe Tonga since their involuntary relocation during the late 1950s in connection with the construction of the first mainstream dam on the Zambezi River."

198 **Shahidian, Hammed** (1996) Iranian Exiles and Sexual Politics: Issues of Gender Relations and Identity. *Journal of Refugee Studies,* 9 (1): 43-72.

"This paper argues that sexual politics among Iranian exiles is a continuation of silenced conflicts between the identities of political activists and social and organizational constraints in Iran. During the initial years of exile, Iran's political conditions remained the preoccupation of the expatriate activists. Later on, after the defeat of the left and its loss of ideological and organizational legitimacy, denied or postponed identities have found a chance to resurface. Sexual politics develops through relationships between individuals and their social environment. First of all, it entails rearrangements of gendered power relations. Second the redistribution of power evokes challenges from expatriates. Third, the host society provides the exiles both with a favorable environment to resolve these conflicts and with new limitations and challenges. Finally, Ideological and political considerations also play an important role in this process. These tensions stem from an attempt on the part of leftist exiles to re-evaluate their past practice of silencing the conflict between their emerging identity and organizational demands, as well as an attempt by female leftist exiles to forge new gender identities and relations."

199 **Shami, Seteney** (1996) Transnationalism and refugee studies: rethinking forced migration and identity in the Middle East. *Journal of Refugee Studies,* 9 (1): 3-26.

"The current enthusiasm in anthropology for the concepts of transnationalism and globalization has significant implications for Refugee Studies as an emergent field, for understandings of the contemporary Middle East, and for the practice of ethnography. In discussing forced migration in the Middle East the argument is made for the importance of retaining the analytical concern for forms and forces of regionalism, while at the same time rethinking them in the light of global changes. This entails a consideration of two problematic topics: Arab nationalism, or rather *al-'uruba* (which translates best as Arabness, and which highlights the identity rather than the ideology); and contemporary Islamic identity, which is better conceptualized as transnationalism rather than fundamentalism. A critical reading of the life history of a Somali woman offers a commentary on the place of ethnography in the context of these analytical concerns, and highlights the problem of using static concepts of Islam and tradition to interpret lives that are transnational."

200 **Sik, Endre** (1990) Policy Networks to Cope with Crisis: The Case of Transylvanian Refugees in Contemporary Hungary. *Innovation,* 3 (4): 729-748.

A study of Transylvanian refugees seeking asylum in contemporary Hungary, based on: a questionnaire survey of 1,367 refugees (of the estimated 34,000 who fled Romania 1987-1990), concerning the circumstances of their flight & their subsequent experiences in Hungary; a survey of 1,000 Hungarians regarding their opinions of this refugee population & of how their government has handled the situation; & a pilot study of the organization of the Hungarian welfare system responsible for the Transylvanians. The situation can be described as chaotic, at best, especially in light of the subsequent collapse of Hungary's communist government. To deal with the crisis, state authorities created a committee-type control structure, which was embedded in the system of interorganizational networks among non-governmental organizations. This policy network may be seen as dualistic, involving both a loose government sector & a new private grass-roots sector with small, independent, very active units. Explanations are offered for the state's choice of this committee structure, as opposed to the "normal" solution in state socialism, ie, a task force or special office. 1 Figure. Adapted from the source document. (Copyright 1992, Sociological Abstracts, Inc., all rights reserved.)

154 REFUGEES, GENDER AND HUMAN SECURITY

201 **Smith-Hefner, Nancy J.** (1996) Acculturative Stress among Amerasian Refugees: Gender and Racial Differences. *Adolescence.*

This paper explores mental health, adjustment, and acculturation among Amerasian refugees as they attempt to adapt to a life in America. The findings do not support other literature on refugees, which indicates that males are more at risk regarding acculturative stress than female refugees. Furthermore, no significant correlation between effective spoken English and employment on stress levels was found. The author discusses implications for social work practice and future research.

202 **Soguk, Nevzat** (1995) Politics of Resistance and Accommodation: Managing Refugee and Immigrant Movements in the Post-Cold War Era. *Current World Leaders,* 38 (2): 102-118.

The author examines the effects on Western countries of recent massive migration waves. He suggests that these waves work both disruptively and recuperatively on the resettlement countries. Responses to the situation (re)shape democracy, stability, security and development, beyond resolving practical problems. This issue is considered to be a choice between moderate accommodation of global realities or confrontation, with nationalist measures foregoing resolution.

203 **Sorenson, John** (1992) Essence and Contingency in the Construction of Nationhood: Transformations of Identity in Ethiopia and Its Diasporas. *Diaspora,* 2 (2): 201-228.

This paper explores the conflicts between national identity and new ethno-national identities within Ethiopia's diaspora population of refugees and emigrants in Canada. Despite their competing national, ethnic, and political identities, all those who have fled Ethiopia as refugees and emigrants have been administered and processed by various institutions as members of one category. However, the paper reveals significant differences between the experiences of political exiles and emigrants whose motive for leaving their homeland was pursuing educational and economic opportunities abroad. There appear to be striking similarities as well, in particular the common feeling of uprooting and dislocation.

204 **Sorenson, John** (1996) Learning to Be Oromo: Nationalist Discourse in the Diaspora. *Social Identities,* 2 (3): 439-467.

Based on observations gathered during Oromo Studies Assoc. meetings, 1989-1994, the role played by Oromo diaspora intellectuals from Ethiopia in promoting a nationalist discourse calling for the creation of an independent state for the Oromo (one of the largest ethnic populations in Africa) is discussed, along with the manner in which their participation in such discursive activities allow them to engage in a reconstruction of their own identities & in the shaping of national & personal senses of the self. It is argued that Oromo nationalists have attempted to deconstruct the dominant discourse of a Greater Ethiopia, which relies on a specific version of history. Instead, Oromo nationalists promote their own version of history. 39 References. Adapted from the source document. (Copyright 1998, Sociological Abstracts, Inc., all rights reserved.)

205 **Spijkerboer, Thomas** (1994) *Women and refugee status: beyond the public/ private distinction.* The Hague: Emancipation Council.

This study deals with the legal position of refugee women, starting from the assumption that refugee law is not gender neutral, at least not in practice. The author tries to answer the question why many of the experiences of refugee women fall outside the scope of the refugee definition, a reality that has serious consequences for women's chances to obtain refugee status. The problem is approached from the perspective of the traditional legal framework (international/refugee law) as well as from legal women's studies. The existing literature on women and refugee law is analysed and directions for new approaches are put forward.

206 **Spring, Anita** (1979) Women and Men as Refugees: Differential Assimilation of Angolan Refugees in Zambia. *Disasters,* 3 (4): 423-428.

The author describes the problems of resettlement faced by Angolans who migrated to Zambia. An analysis of the effects of sex and age on resettlement show that Angolan women achieve success more quickly than men; younger ones divorce refugee husbands for established settlers. Men, often without a wife, endure poverty. In spite of being stereotyped by Zambian residents as culturally and politically backward, Angolans apply their medical skills and native health lore. Women health practitioners are more successful than male ritualists.

207 **Steen, Ann-Belinda** (1993) *Varieties of the Tamil refugee experience in Denmark and England.* Copenhagen: Minority Studies.

This study which deals with the Tamil diaspora is based on anthropological fieldwork among Tamil refugees in London and Denmark (1988-89). The author argues for a rethinking and widening of refugee research, basing her arguments on the challenges that the refugee phenomenon offers to western governments and European politics, as well as to academia and traditional anthropology. This is illustrated by an examination of the impact of refugee policy on Tamils in the above mentioned communities, as well as through issues of 'Tamilness' and the social and cultural changes related to that notion in exile.

208 **Stepputat, Finn** (1994) Repatriation and the Politics of Space: The Case of the Mayan Diaspora and Return Movement. *Journal of Refugee Studies,* 7 (2-3): 175-185.

"This paper explores the meanings of return and repatriation among Guatemalan refugees who are now returning from a decade of exile in Mexico. The analysis applies a transnational perspective which does not take the attachment of people to certain places and territories as a natural given. Rather, it is argued, the dynamics of flight and return should be explored in terms of the 'politics of space' of the nation state, that is, the development and application of techniques of power for the control of territories and populations."

209 **Sullivan, Kathleen** (1996) Constructing 'La Casa de la Mujer': the Guatamalan refugee women and the midwives of Monja Blanca in El Porvenir border camp, Mexico. In W. Giles, H. Moussa, & P. van Esterik (eds) *Development and diaspora: gender and the refugee experience.* Canada: Artemis Enterprises, pp. 268-279.

"In this paper the women's struggle for a legitimate space is manifested in the construction of La Casa de la Mujer (The Women's House), where women can share their concerns regarding health, human rights and other social issues. As protagonists of change, their strategies, as described by the author, challenge the western capitalist notion of the gendered division of labour and the artificial divide between the domestic/private and the public. While the women are seen as the conservers of tradition and transmitters of culture, they also are able to adapt traditions, beliefs and customs as they confront new challenges in their daily lives."

210 **Tapp, Nicholas** (1988) The reformation of culture: Hmong refugees from Laos. *Journal of Refugee Studies,* 1 (1).

"This essay demonstrates how an oral tradition may encapsulate certain aspects of changing social circumstances within the context of a felt past. The first part describes the situation of Hmong refugees in a Thai refugee-camp. An examination of the emergence of a revivalist movement among Hmong refugees in Thailand follows. The third part analyses an oral legend in the context of the refugee situation. The final part considers the material problems of Hmong refugees overseas in the light of their cultural traditions. Fieldwork was conducted in a White Hmong village in North Thailand for 18 month in 1981-1982, and subsequently for shorter periods in France and USA. While not representing the fruits of extensive fieldwork in refugee communities, the paper aims to present a compressed and informed account of some problems now confronting Hmong refugees with regard to their cultural traditions, studied more extensively in the village-site."

211 **Toshchenko, Zhan T.** (1994) *Refugees in Russia as the Problem of Social Disaster.* Paper for the International Sociological Association,Moscow.

Refugees in Russia present a great social problem after the collapse of the USSR, affecting the economic stability, social welfare, & everyday life of population. At present 25 million Russians live in the former republics of the USSR, 2 million of whom are refugees. Public opinion polls show that 6 million of them want to leave the former republics for Russia, primarily because of the gap of economic links, social shortcomings, political instability, & the complex influence of the national consciousness. War conflicts, the struggle for political power, the growth of crime, & violence, & national chauvinism render many refugees unsure of their own & their children's future. Consequences of this social disaster are outlined: many refugees have lost houses, jobs, material & spiritual welfare; distrust among the nationalities is growing; & there is economic catastrophe in the republics in Middle Asia, because the intellectuals in industries, science, & culture leave for Russia. There is also the danger of civil war & great political economic instability for a long time. (Copyright 1994, Sociological Abstracts, Inc., all rights reserved.)

212 **Toth, O.** (1994) Transylvanian refugee women in Hungary: 1989. *Gains and losses: women and transition in Eastern and Central Europe.* Bucharest: pp. 95-107.

"This article describes an in-depth sociological investigation undertaken in March 1989 of 1,367 persons, 557 of whom were women, who had recently emigrated from Romanian Transylvania to Hungary. The aim of the study was to determine if women emigrants fared differently from male emigrants and whether or not these women and men who entered Hungary legally fared differently from those who entered illegally. The degree of successful adaptation to life in Hungary was measured for men and women, both il-legal and legal entrants, according to the criteria of success in finding em-ployment, success in obtaining private housing, ability to initiate and/or to maintain satisfactory mental health. Although striking differences between men and women with regard to success according to these criteria were regis-tered, the immigrants from Transylvania as a group were generally optimis-tic about their futures in Hungary."

213 **Tran, Qui P.** (1993) Contemporary Vietnamese American Feminine Writing: Exile and Home. *Amerasia Journal,* 19 (3): 71-83.

Two grand themes – exile & home – are apparent in recent writings by Vietnamese-American female authors, several of which are described here. Home carries a highly emotional meaning for Vietnamese-American women, associated with the mother(land). The sense of exile is particularly poignant, because these women left Vietnam as adults, & had major prob-lems with resettlement in a Western culture. Within the theme of exile, the issues of existence, female sexuality, & female responses to cultural & soci-etal impressions are treated. The themes of exile & home, originating after 1975 in the works of Vietnamese refugees to the West, show no sign of abat-ing in popularity, because they provide the means for the authors to come to terms with their present realities, to create new lives, & to have faith in their nationality. M. Pflum (Copyright 1994, Sociological Abstracts, Inc., all rights reserved.)

214 **Tran, Thanh V., & Thang D. Nguyen** (1994) Gender and Satisfaction with the Host Society among Indochinese Refugees. *International Migra-tion Review,* 28 (2[106]): 323-337.

"This study examines gender differences in satisfaction with the host society (swhs) in terms of satisfaction with housing, neighborhood and life. A sample of 1,384 respondents aged 17 to 73 was selected from the 1982 na-tional survey of economic self-sufficiency of Indochinese refugees. Regres-sion analysis revealed that for men: 1) satisfaction with housing was influ-enced by age upon arrival in the United States and financial problems; 2) sat-isfaction with neighborhood was influenced by age upon arrival in the United States, lack of health care, financial problems and ethnicity; and 3) satisfaction with life was influenced by age upon arrival in the United States, employment, lack of health care, financial problems, and English ability. For women, the regression analysis revealed slightly different results: 1) satis-faction with housing was influenced by urban background in country of origin and length of residence in the United States; 2) satisfaction with neighborhood was influenced by financial problems, education in country of origin, and ethnicity; and 3) satisfaction with life had no statistical significant relationship with selected independent variables. Gender and age had significant interaction effect on satisfaction with housing, neighborhood and life. Gender and education had significant interaction effect on satisfaction with neighborhood. Implications for practice and future research are discussed."

215 **Turton, David** (1996) Migrants & refugees : a Mursi case study. In T. Allen (ed) *In search of cool ground : war, flight & homecoming in northeast Africa.* London: James Currey, pp. 96-110.

This paper is based on anthropological fieldwork carried out over the past 25 years among the Mursi, a herding and cultivating people of southwestern Ethiopia. The author describes two cases of population displacement that took place in the area: First, a drought-induced – 'voluntary' – migration from northern Mursiland to the Mago valley in 1979, and second a war-induced – forced – migration of the entire population of two southern Mursi territorial sections, Ariholi and Gongulobibi in 1987. The different characters of the two periods of flight imply that for the Mago migrants, return would mean failure, whereas for the Ariholi and Gongulobibi refugees, success. The author intends to induce critical reflection upon the assumption that the very word 'displacement' implies that all human populations 'belong' in a certain place by examining what the two movements meant to the Mursi themselves.

216 UNHCR (1985) *Refugee women: selected and annotated bibliography.* Geneva: UNHCR, CDR.

"This revised and updated edition of the United Nations High Commissioner for Refugees (UNHCR) 1985 bibliography on women refugees covers materials written between 1985 and 1989. It includes 214 abstracts organized in nine sections: international concern and protection; discrimination and violence against women; refugee camps; integration, customs and traditions; social services; education and training; employment and income-generation; health and resource materials. Publishers' addresses are provided. The bibliography includes extensive listing of documents from the United Nations and UNHCR." (taken from Neuwirth & Vincent [1997])

160   REFUGEES, GENDER AND HUMAN SECURITY

217 **UNHCR** (1989) *Refugee women: selected and annotated bibliography (revised and updated version)*. Geneva: UNHCR, CDR.

"A joint publication by UNHCR and the Refugee Policy Group, this bibliography includes 139 abstracts of articles and reports on refugee women. The entries stem from the UNHCR Refugee Documentation Centre's Refugee Abstracts data base, the Refugee Policy Group and other international data bases, and are the results of enquiries with libraries, documentation centres, publishers and refugee assisting organizations in a number of countries. Entries are organized under nine main categories, ranging from international concern and protection to employment and income-generation; health; and resource materials. Relevant index terms and publishers' addresses are included."(taken from Neuwirth & Vincent [1997])

218 **Valtonen, Kathleen** (1994) Adaptation of Vietnamese refugees in Finland. *Journal of Refugee Studies,* 7 (1): 63-78.

"This study examines the life conditions of Vietnamese refugees resettled in Turku in order to understand the nature and pattern of their social adaptation. The research was qualitative and based on in-depth interviews of 57 adults. The heterogeneous refugee group comprises highly cohesive subgroups exhibiting interaction characteristics very similar to extended family interaction: intensity of contacts with responsibility-type roles, as well as deep informal involvement in times of crisis. Sub-groups seem imprinted with the structure and roles of the extended family. The ethnic group seem imprinted to be rebuilding the traditional support network in the resettlement environment, guided by role-related selection criteria. High intra-group interaction indicates maintenance of cultural and group social identity. Secondary contacts occurred in the workplace, at school and with 'friend families'. Thus, on the basis of Berry's (1988) acculturation model, the adaptation pattern of the Vietnamese group was found to be that of integration."

219 **Voutira, Eftihia et al.** (1995) *Improving social and gender planning in emergency operations.* Oxford: RSP.

The RSP, Oxford University, was invited by the World Food Programme (WFP) to conduct a desk review of existing models of food distribution in emergency situations as well as in protracted emergencies. Findings are put down in this elaborate report. Its main focus is to consider food distribution practices in the light of the need to improve the status of women, to ensure their access to food, to increase their participation in decision-making in general and particularly in terms of food distribution in emergency situations. The main findings and recommendations are outlined in the last chapter of the report.

220 **Waal, Alex de** (1988) Refugees and the creation of famine: the case of Dar Masalit, Sudan. *Journal of Refugee Studies,* 1 (2).

"Western Sudan and Chad were hit by famine in 1984/5. Dar Masalit stands out as a 'pocket' of exceptionally severe and prolonged famine. This is related to the fact that the area hosted 120,000 Chadian refugees at the time. Comparative data show that population movements of comparable size in this area need not cause famine. There were two other critical differences in this case. One factor was insecurity in Chad, which prevented the refugees returning home to plant in the rains of 1985. The second was the nature of the assistance programme. This was based on notions of 'refugeehood' that were inappropriate to western Sudan, which has its own conceptions of 'refugeehood' and a long history of dealing with refugees. The assistance programme restricted the mobility and hindered the integration of the refugee population, and thereby maintained them in an economically fragile area, contributing to the disaster."

221 **Wallace, Tina** (1994) Saharawi Women: 'Between Ambition and Suffering'. *Focus on Gender,* 2 (1): 50-53.

Drawing from papers presented at a conference on Saharawi women refugees organized in the House of Commons by One World Action, Oct 1993, it is argued that stereotypes of long-term refugee African women are negative even though many have done impressive work in health, education, & agriculture. It is essential to listen to & talk to refugees, look at their rights, & support women during the transition back to their homes. Saharawi women have been able to uphold their traditions, establish social cohesiveness, & control day-to-day camp operations. Now they are planning for the future & hope to enshrine the rights they have gained in refugee camps into a new constitution. 2 References. V. Wagener (Copyright 1995, Sociological Abstracts, Inc., all rights reserved.)

222 **Walsum, Sarah van** (1994) Mixed metaphors: the nation and the family. In K. and F. von Benda-Beckmann & H. Marks (eds) *Coping with insecurity: an 'underall' perspective on social security in the Third World.* Special Issue Focaal 22/23, pp. 199-218.

This paper deals with the security position of migrants in the Netherlands. Different pictures are drawn of two people born as Dutch citizens on the other side of the Atlantic – Surinam and Canada – now living in Amsterdam. The author discusses the concept of nationality in Dutch immigration law and in the country's policies on ethnic minorities, and terms it an exclusionary criterion. She continues by examining the politics and metaphors of (national) space, place and the family and the interrelations between these. In the concluding paragraph, the author speaks of the nation and the family as bones of contention, arguing how an important element of distinction between 'the Dutch' and 'the others' has proven to be the family and associated gender roles.

223 **Weighill, Marie-Louise** (1997) Palestinians in Lebanon: the politics of assistance. *Journal of Refugee Studies,* 10 (3): 294-313.

"This paper explores the extent to which political considerations have affected both the planning and delivery of assistance to Palestinian refugees in Lebanon. In the first section a historical overview of Palestinian assistance covers the creation and consolidation of UNRWA, the rise and collapse of an autonomous Palestinian assistance structure, and the post-civil war 'policy vacuum'. The second section discusses the connection between the receipt of organized international assistance and the loss of political and socio-economic autonomy for the refugee community; the unique assistance structure created for the Palestinian refugees which has amalgamated the two distinct elements of legal protection and socio-economic assistance; and the impact of the concept of *tawteen* (loosely, assimilation) on the nature and extent of assistance design. Finally, the paper discusses the impact of the current peace process on refugee assistance, and offers recommendations for the separation of refugee assistance from the pursuance and enforcement of Palestinians' legal prerogatives and assistance options that promote both Palestinian autonomy and mutually beneficial links with the host society."

224 **Weist, Katherine M.** (1995) Development Refugees: Africans, Indians and the Big Dams. *Journal of Refugee Studies,* 8 (2): 163-184.

"People involuntarily removed due to construction of development projects undergo grief, cultural involution, and fundamental restructuring of their lives. Drawing upon the processual model of Elizabeth Colson and Thayer Scudder, this paper analyses the effects which removal had on five populations, two in Africa and three in North America. The Gwembe Tonga, Egyptian Nubians, and Three Affiliated Tribes of Fort Berthold, Seneca, and James Bay Cree all underwent massive changes with the inundation of their lands due to the construction of large hydroelectric dams. All underwent a process of grief and all resisted their resettlement. Comparative analysis indicates, however, that the resettlement process differed in terms of each society's incorporation into the larger national arena, compensation given for lands lost, coping mechanisms, and the time period in which the resettlement occurred."

225 **Williams, Holly A.** (1990) Family functioning in refugee camps: a review of the literature. *Human Organization,* 49 (2): 100-109.
"This article examines how families respond to the experience of being in refugee camps. The author tries to discern common behaviours that reflect how families in crisis cope. She gives an overview of literature on families within the context of the pre-migration period and the camp experience, and states that the fabric of family life begins to be dramatically altered during pre-migration periods, with serious repercussions to all involved. The social organization and the structural elements of the family are analyzed in regard to external conditions that affect them. The author posits that the refugee family experiences a major power shift from internal control to external control over future life decisions." (adapted from Neuwirth & Vincent [1997])

226 **Wilson, Fiona** (1997) Recuperation in the Peruvian Andes. In C. Kay (ed) *Globalisation, competitiveness and human security.* London: Frank Cass, pp. 231-245.
"Violent conflict is highly damaging for human security and the entire fabric of regional society. Individuals and groups confront situations that are unpredictable, threatening and impoverishing in material and cultural terms, and many communities are dislocated and deterritorialised. But conflict and instability do not in themselves constitute useful points of departure for the analysis of post-conflict situations. In this contribution I seek to highlight which actors, social relations and constellations of power come to prominence in the aftermath of violent conflict; examine the tensions arising from the different meanings given to 'recuperation'; and investigate the spatial practice of social actors taking part in processes of recuperation. This

164   REFUGEES, GENDER AND HUMAN SECURITY

contribution builds on an ongoing fieldwork study in a province of the Peruvian Central Andes."

227 **Wilson, Ken B.** (1992) *Internally displaced, refugees and returnees from and in Mozambique.* Stockholm: SIDA.

This study provides an overview and examination of research undertaken so far on forced migrations from and within Mozambique. It includes investigations of the causes and nature of the displacements and the survival strategies of the displaced people, as well as research on the impact of forced migration on the hosting areas and the nature and impact of assistance programmes. In its references, the study includes the papers and publications of the Refugee Studies Programme Documentation Centre on displaced, returnee and refugee Mozambicans.

228 **Wilson, Ken B.** (1992) Enhancing refugees' own food acquisition strategies. *Journal of Refugee Studies,* 5 (3/4).

"Improved support for the nutritional needs of refugees can best be achieved through strengthening refugees' existing livelihood and food acquisition strategies, recognizing their capacities to be economic agents and to meet their own needs. A priority would be removing the constraints on refugees of existing policies and systems of administration which often weaken refugees' access to resources and markets, especially through distorting population distribution (through camps) and by imposing numerous petty restrictions on activities. Application of economic concepts to food aid disbursement suggests that the distribution of cash, perhaps alongside programmes to maintain food in local markets, would be a better way to secure refugee entitlement. It is further argued that cash provision would reduce logistical burdens on agencies and have more developmental affects, although it also has its shortcomings. It is time for carefully monitored experimentation with such new approaches."

229 **Winland, Daphne N.** (1994) Christianity and Community: Conversion and Adaptation among Hmong Refugee Women. *Canadian Journal of Sociology / Cahiers canadiens de sociologie,* 19 (1): 21-45.

Data obtained via participant observation & interviews, 1985-1989, are drawn on to examine the role of Christian conversion on the early adjustment experience of 43 Laotian Hmong refugee women in Ontario. It is demonstrated that this transition from a traditionally animist & preliterate past did not result in the wholesale abandonment of Hmong practices & beliefs, but rather in a dynamic relationship of custom & innovation. Women in particular turned to the Hmong Christian church (Mennonite) as a resource for empowerment, but also to maintain key Hmong social practices & values. The church proved to be a valuable resource in helping these refugee women cope more effectively with the constraints of gender & minority status. 71 References. Adapted from the source document. (Copyright 1994, Sociological Abstracts, Inc., all rights reserved.)

230 **Wong, Diana** (1989) The Semantics of Migration. *SOJOURN*, 4 (2): 275-285.
An exploration of the context in which international migrants came to be categorized as immigrants or refugees. The emergence of migrants is discussed as a "discursive fact," which has assumed specific parameters only in the fairly recent past. It is shown how both sending & receiving countries impose their definitions of migration on the migrants. The construction of the labels illegal immigrant & refugee is discussed, along with how they have been integrated into the general sociological, legal, & popular discourse. 20 References. (Copyright 1990, Sociological Abstracts, Inc., all rights reserved.)

231 **Wong, Diana** (1991) Asylum as a relationship of otherness: a study of asylum holders in Nuremberg, Germany. *Journal of Refugee Studies*, 4 (2): 150-163.
"In this paper, it is argued that the analysis of the experience of exile and asylum should be located on a double axis of presence and absence, as well as in the medium of time, both in its quantitative and qualitative aspects. The point of departure for the analysis is a rejection of the integration problematic prevailing in the sociology of migration, employing in its stead the perspective of the relationship of otherness as a heuristic device. The paper draws upon textual material generated by narrative interviews with asylum holders from Eritrea, Iran and Afghanistan presently living in the city of Nuremberg in south Germany."

232 **Xenos, Nicholas** (1993) Refugees: The Modern Political Condition. *Alternatives*, 18 (4): 419-430.
The Haitian boat people & other recent refugee groups are cited as examples of how people wishing to flee a repressive country become pawns in a struggle between nation-states. Implicit in the response to refugees are the dismissal of the individual's right to asylum, & the affirmation of the state's claim to sovereignty & absolute control over its territory, as well as its spe-

cific national identity. For refugees, national identity confers rootedness. Thus, the concepts of statelessness & homelessness both apply to refugee status: the refugee's problem is in establishing a home (identity), not just in being denied a homeland (a space in a state). (Copyright 1994, Sociological Abstracts, Inc., all rights reserved.)

233 **Yee, Barbara W. K.** (1992) Elders in Southeast Asian Refugee Families. *Generations,* 16 (3): 24-27.

This paper reveals through secondary research that the situation of elderly Southeast Asian refugees in the US is very different from what they expected. Lacking the extended families from their homelands they face isolation due to language barriers and the Americanisation of (grand)children, altered gender roles and different definitions of aging. Instead of providing land and material support, they now can only offer child care and feel deprived of due respect. Those living with their families are better off and young elderly women are more integrated but as they age, they often get isolated.

234 **Young, Helen** (1992) A case study of the Chadian refugees in Western Sudan: the impact of the food assessment mission. *Journal of Refugee Studies,* 5 (3/4).

"This case study of providing food assistance to Chadian refugees in Western Sudan illustrates some of the problems that are common to many refugee situations throughout Africa. The first part of the paper describes the initial emergency in 1985 and 1986 when refugee camps were established. The second part describes how refugee food requirements are determined by the annual Food Assessment Mission (a joint undertaking by the World Food Programme, UN High Commissioner for Refugees and the host government). The inherent weaknesses in a system that has no clear procedures for such an important function are examined. Finally, the failure of the system to meet its agreed commitments for food assistance for refugees is examined. Despite this failure, refugees were able to develop livelihoods which enabled them to make up the shortfall in the rations provided."

235 **Zakharia, Leila, & Samia Tabari** (1997) Health, work opportunities and attitudes: a review of Palestinian women's situation in Lebanon. *Journal of Refugee Studies,* 10 (3): 411-429.

"This study of 1,501 Palestinian women refugees, 80 per cent of them living in camps, and all within the age range 15-60 years, examines their reproductive health, together with the health of their children; their circumstances of employment; and their attitudes and preferences in these aspects of their lives. Early marriage, high fertility and inadequate contraceptive advice meant that most women had more children than they would have wished, and were burdened with child care and domestic duties. At the same time, a high proportion were also employed, most often in unskilled poorly paid jobs. A preference could be seen for later marriage and further education, with the improved job opportunities that this would bring."

236 **Zetter, Roger** (1991) Labelling refugees: forming and transforming a bureaucratic identity. *Journal of Refugee Studies*, 4 (1): 39-62.
"This essay examines how and with what consequences people become labelled as refugees within the context of public policy practices. Conceptual and operational limitations to the existing definition of refugees are noted. These, the paper contends, derive from the absence of a systematic study of labelling processes in the donative policy discourse associated with refugees. The paper outlines the conceptual tools of bureaucratic labelling – stereotyping, conformity, designation, identity disaggregation and political/power relationships. These tools are then deployed to analyse empirical data collected from a large refugee population in Cyprus, supplemented by selective secondary research data on various African refugee populations. The analysis proceeds in three parts. First the formation of the label is considered in which stereotyped identities are translated into bureaucratically assumed needs. The label thus takes on a selective, materialist meaning. Alienating distinctions emerge by the creation of different categories of refugee deemed necessary to prioritize need. Next, reformation of the label is considered. The evidence shows how latent and manifest processes of institutional action and programme delivery, reinforce a disaggregated model of identity; in this case disturbing distinctions are made between refugee and non-refugee. Third, the paper considers how labels assume, often conflicting, politicized meanings, for both labelled and labellers. The paper concludes by emphasizing: the extreme vulnerability of refugees to imposed labels; the importance of symbolic meaning; the dynamic nature of the identity; and, most fundamentally of all, the non-participatory nature and powerlessness of refugees in these processes."

168   REFUGEES, GENDER AND HUMAN SECURITY

237 **Zetter, Roger** (1994) The Greek-Cypriot Refugees: Perceptions of Return under Conditions of Protracted Exile. *International Migration Review,* 28 (2[106]): 307-322.

"Constituting a crucial element in the search for a permanent solution to the Cyprus problem, the needs and aspirations of 180,000 refugees are examined in this article. Of the three durable solutions to the refugee crises, repatriation has consistently been advocated as the only option for the Cypriot situation. Contrasting the images of temporariness and permanency of exile, the article examines the extent to which the refugees, in the light of the dramatic social and economic changes that have taken place in the refugee community since the exodus of 1974, might perceive of return as their sole feasible or potential objective. The article argues that the ambiguous identity of the refugees, as both insiders and outsiders, and the protracted political uncertainty of their status give contradictory messages about the likely scale, processes, and success of their return."

238 **Zetter, Roger** (1995) Incorporation and Exclusion: The Life Cycle of Malawi's Refugee Assistance Program. *World Development,* 23 (10): 1653-1667.

An examination of the assistance provision to 1.2 million Mozambican refugees in Malawi identifies three phases. An innovative model of assistance delivery, integrating refugees & hosts in a development-oriented program, was established in the early phases, avoiding the parallel structures of orthodox relief operations. Within the context of its political economy, the government of Malawi successfully mediated competing interests. Incrementally, the host government lost autonomy; this is explained in terms of pressures to internationalize & diversify the program & the adoption of a conventional relief model focusing only on refugees & emergency assistance. With extensive repatriation, the program is winding down. The lessons learned are discussed. 72 References. Adapted from the source document. (Copyright 1996, Sociological Abstracts, Inc., all rights reserved.)

239 **Zetter, Roger** (1996) Refugee Survival and NGO Project Assistance: Mozambican Refugees in Malawi. *Community Development Journal,* 31 (3): 214-229.

"This paper retrospectively examines the impact of developmentally orientated NGO projects on Mozambican refugee survival in Malawi. Five limitations are elaborated: unresponsiveness to local economic conditions and skills; inadequate methods of recruitment; production, business plan and marketing constraints and lack of sustainability; limited participation and the imposition of management ideologies; gender inequalities and inadequate gender-related policies. The analysis of these shortcomings offer guidance to the mobilisation of development projects in future large-scale refugee situations."

240 **Zlotnik, Hania** (1990) International Migration Policies and the Status of Female Migrants. *International Migration Review,* 24 (2[90]): 372-381.

This is a report of the problems discussed at a conference on internal migrants – 48% of whom were women then – organised by the UN Population Division in Italy in March 1990. Conclusions were that the implementation of migration regulations is often affected by stereotypical images of sex roles in the country of origin resulting in indirect discrimination in admitting countries. To fight this recommendations were given, ranging from consciousness raising to affirmative action and guidelines for government action like modifying discriminatory regulations and increasing awareness of vulnerable groups, and ensuring gender-equal access to the labour market, social services and legalization.

241 **Zolberg, Aristide R., Astri Suhrke, & Sergio Aguayo** (1986) International Factors in the Formation of Refugee Movements. *International Migration Review,* 20 (2): 151-169.

"On the basis of detailed case studies by the authors of the principal refugee flows generated in Asia, Africa, and Latin America from approximately 1960 to the present, it was found that international factors often intrude both directly and indirectly on the major types of social conflict that trigger refugee flows, and tend to exacerbate their effects. Refugees are also produced by conflicts that are manifestly international, but which are themselves often related to internal social conflict among the antagonists. Theoretical frameworks for the analysis of the causes of refugee movements must therefore reflect the transnational character of the processes involved. This paper sets forth such a framework and points to the policy implications of the proposed reconceptualization."

Subject Index

Forced Migration

refugees
returnees   7, 8, 9, 34, 46, 82, 117, 125, 131, 208, 227
internally displaced persons   42, 53, 84, 106, 111, 134, 194, 195, 227, 240
stayees   31
development refugees   42, 197, 224
illegality   38, 56, 150, 212
repatriation   1, 8, 9, 14, 34, 46, 57, 74, 78, 91, 117, 131, 166, 173, 180, 196, 208, 237
resettlement   1, 8, 9, 43, 45, 54, 96, 106, 108, 112, 139, 160, 172, 175, 176
host society   1, 5, 7, 8, 9, 16, 18, 26, 27, 35, 59, 76, 83, 87, 97, 99, 118, 121, 126, 127, 133, 140, 180, 193, 198, 200, 202, 214, 227
globalisation   19, 38, 89, 107, 110, 139, 148, 189, 199, 202, 241
refugee regime   51, 63, 67, 85, 90, 139
refugee label   51, 129, 134, 141, 151, 188, 189, 203, 215, 220, 230, 236

Human Security

personal security
– physical insecurity   4, 17, 33, 41, 111, 163, 165, 211
– gender insecurity   4, 17, 20, 21, 22, 25, 41, 48, 55, 57, 58, 66, 73, 74, 79, 99, 102, 122, 165, 167, 177
– identity   15, 16, 25, 33, 40, 47, 73, 103, 104, 129, 149, 150, 152, 172, 173, 199, 208, 237
– ethnic identity   39, 40, 54, 59, 68, 74, 122, 123, 124, 128, 136, 140, 153, 163, 165, 171, 194, 207
– national identity   47, 51, 64, 150, 203, 204, 232
– belonging   7, 16, 51, 65, 70, 73, 78, 82, 122, 142, 150, 168, 172, 173, 203, 213, 215, 231, 232, 234
– kinship   32, 81, 133, 135, 170
health security
– physical health   37, 44, 54, 72, 74, 76, 86, 94, 137, 175, 181, 206, 209, 214, 216, 217, 235
– mental / psychological health   3, 4, 8, 9, 10, 24, 29, 30, 48, 61, 69, 101, 120, 136, 154, 155, 159, 160, 174, 175, 178, 183, 201, 212
– trauma   4, 10, 24, 29, 61, 105, 120, 132, 154, 183

political security
- national security   1, 56, 67, 89,
  95, 232
- nationalism   74, 75, 149, 165,
  199, 204, 211, 222
- regional security   1, 56, 89, 95,
  107, 158, 226, 241
- state oppression   4, 73, 79, 89,
  95, 108, 165, 186, 194, 208, 232
legal security
- human rights   13, 22, 38, 49, 53,
  66, 67, 79, 80, 90, 130, 134, 177,
  205
- international law   13, 20, 21, 22,
  41, 44, 49, 66, 67, 90, 113, 134,
  143, 144, 146, 149, 156, 177
- protection   20, 21, 22, 38, 41, 53,
  90, 113, 131, 134, 169, 196, 216,
  217, 219, 223
- refugee / asylum policy   13, 20,
  21, 22, 44, 51, 56, 63, 66, 69, 71,
  74, 90, 96, 112, 113, 127, 130, 143,
  144, 156, 189, 205, 207, 222
- gender-based persecution   20,
  21, 22, 41, 57, 66, 79, 108, 112, 113,
  143, 144, 146, 156, 177, 205
food security
- food insecurity   35, 37, 43, 65,
  67, 74, 133, 219
- food assistance   2, 8, 9, 35, 36,
  85, 88, 91, 219, 220, 228, 234
- famine   23, 215, 220
economic security
- economic insecurity   5, 8, 9, 11,
  26, 33, 35, 43, 44, 54, 58, 67, 79,
  117, 119, 126, 127, 157, 180, 193,
  211, 223

- employment   5, 43, 46, 58, 98,
  99, 106, 119, 147, 157, 160, 201,
  212, 214, 216, 217, 235
- housing & land   19, 67, 125,
  212, 214
- education   2, 12, 44, 72, 80, 99,
  114, 160, 192, 201, 216, 217, 235
- social security networks & systems   8, 9, 31, 32, 92, 116, 135,
  190, 191, 200, 218

Gender

gender roles / relations   12, 18, 25,
  28, 33, 36, 40, 45, 50, 69, 74, 97,
  98, 108, 109, 116, 124, 128, 137,
  138, 145, 153, 161, 172, 178, 190,
  191, 194, 206, 218, 233
gender concepts / symbols   18, 28,
  33, 40, 46, 75, 81, 97, 102, 124,
  137, 173, 194
gender inequality   2, 6, 12, 35, 36,
  37, 44, 45, 54, 75, 80, 109, 125,
  145, 157, 209, 229, 239
gender identity   21, 33, 40, 47, 64,
  73, 74, 161, 186, 194, 198, 213
sexual violence   4, 17, 20, 21, 22,
  24, 41, 66, 74, 79, 113, 146, 156,
  161, 163, 205, 216, 217
female headed households
family life   6, 54, 55, 69, 98, 159,
  185, 192, 222, 225
marriage   6, 25, 33, 55, 109, 191, 235
honour   4, 128, 146, 198
women's groups   11, 47, 93, 186,
  209

Subject Index

Human Agency

experience   2, 4, 6, 15, 28, 30, 34, 60, 61, 70, 71, 79, 96, 104, 108, 109, 129, 164, 167, 185, 187, 194
agency   25, 27, 34, 35, 36, 37, 39, 40, 45, 47, 50, 59, 60, 62, 70, 71, 73 74, 96, 97, 98, 102, 115, 116, 131, 132, 133, 161, 164, 171, 172, 174, 182, 185, 187, 194, 206, 209, 221
vulnerability   23, 50, 167, 168
dependency syndrome   8, 85, 88, 115, 121
coping   8, 11, 14, 61, 91, 92, 105, 120, 155, 185, 225, 227, 234
self reliance   35, 75, 83, 84, 85, 115, 119, 121, 170, 190, 195, 228
participation   14, 25, 41, 45, 74, 76, 88, 93, 99, 100, 107, 169, 181, 195, 228, 239
resistance   25, 93, 94, 132, 165, 172, 176, 186
activism   19, 26, 34, 47, 73, 75, 84, 93, 98, 108, 165, 192, 198
religious practices and experiences   25, 32, 40, 68, 73, 86, 124, 152, 229

Age

children   16, 69, 112, 159
adolescents   10, 16, 39, 40, 136, 142, 201
elderly   54, 81, 138, 233

Changing security

integration   8, 27, 33, 63, 82, 97, 114, 126, 127, 216, 217, 231
reintegration   14, 34, 46, 78, 158, 166, 226
acculturation   15, 18, 126
adjustment   27, 28, 33, 39, 50, 54, 59, 64, 82, 83, 99, 124, 138, 147, 201, 213, 218, 229
social / culture change   8, 25, 28, 33, 40, 50, 60, 68, 78, 80, 87, 97, 101, 108, 116, 123, 124, 128, 136, 138, 152, 197, 199, 210, 237

Aid

relief aid   2, 8, 9, 23, 36, 37, 42, 76, 77, 85, 86, 88, 89, 91, 115, 180, 196, 220, 223, 227
disaster relief   8, 9
development aid   8, 9, 14, 42, 77, 107, 139, 166, 169, 195, 219, 238, 239
gender-specific assistance   41, 45, 50, 58, 69, 100, 106, 114, 119, 169, 181, 219, 221, 240
UNHCR   8, 9, 22, 85, 91, 139, 175, 177, 196, 216, 217

Research methods and practice

feminist theory   65, 74, 79, 98, 100, 102, 168
research methodology   40, 55, 85, 87, 103, 168

personal account 70, 71, 82, 104, 130, 168, 184, 213

life history 60, 64, 103, 167, 172, 174, 182, 184, 199

anthropology 52, 86, 87, 110, 149

Region

Northeast Africa 1, 8, 9, 10, 11, 14, 24, 25, 33, 50, 74, 76, 77, 81, 85, 86, 91, 106, 114, 115, 116, 117, 121, 127, 150, 151, 160, 161, 166, 172, 173, 177, 180, 196, 203, 204, 215, 220, 234

Central & West Africa 32, 62, 67, 92, 133, 138

Southern Africa 2, 33, 35, 36, 58, 74, 119, 135, 145, 158, 197, 206, 227, 238, 239

Latin America 4, 27, 33, 39, 79, 104, 108, 109, 226

Central America 34, 40, 59, 60, 74, 84, 89, 93, 98, 125, 131, 162, 186, 208, 209

Caribbean 28, 40, 232

USA 12, 18, 28, 39, 59, 83, 98, 104, 124, 128, 138, 147, 156, 160, 161, 170, 171, 178, 179, 201, 214, 229, 233

Canada 13, 20, 24, 25, 74, 99, 100, 101, 143, 144, 172, 203

Europe 5, 6, 11, 16, 17, 23, 26, 27, 31, 33, 38, 40, 47, 63, 68, 73, 74, 78, 81, 108, 109, 122, 132, 136, 142, 152, 153, 163, 185, 191, 200, 207, 211, 212, 218, 231, 236, 237

Middle East 4, 5, 6 , 7, 33, 44, 47, 73, 75, 78, 82, 105, 152, 153, 192, 193, 198, 199, 223, 235

Central Asia 40, 57, 178, 211

South Asia 33, 111, 119, 194, 195, 207

Southeast Asia 12, 18, 19, 33, 40, 45, 46, 55, 56, 61, 71, 74, 83, 94, 96, 99, 123, 124, 128, 129, 130, 136, 137, 167, 168, 170, 171, 179, 190, 210, 213, 214, 218, 229, 233

Australia / New Zealand 16

Curriculum Vitae

Ellen Lammers (1972) is a graduate from the School of Oriental and African Studies, University of London (Medical Anthropology), and from the Free University of Amsterdam (Cultural Anthropology). She has been working as a junior researcher at INDRA, University of Amsterdam, since 1997. There she helped set up the Interdisciplinary Researchers Group Refugee Issues, which now comprises more than 80 researchers from all Dutch universities and research institutes. She also participated as a member of the steering committee in the organisation of the international conference *Loss and Recovery: Refugees and the Transformation of Society*, scheduled for April 1999. Ellen Lammers will start her Ph.D. research in Uganda in the course of 1999, focusing on issues of gender and human security in the lives of young urban refugees in Kampala.